AF594828

GREAT GOYA ETCHINGS

THE PROVERBS, THE TAUROMAQUIA AND THE BULLS OF BORDEAUX

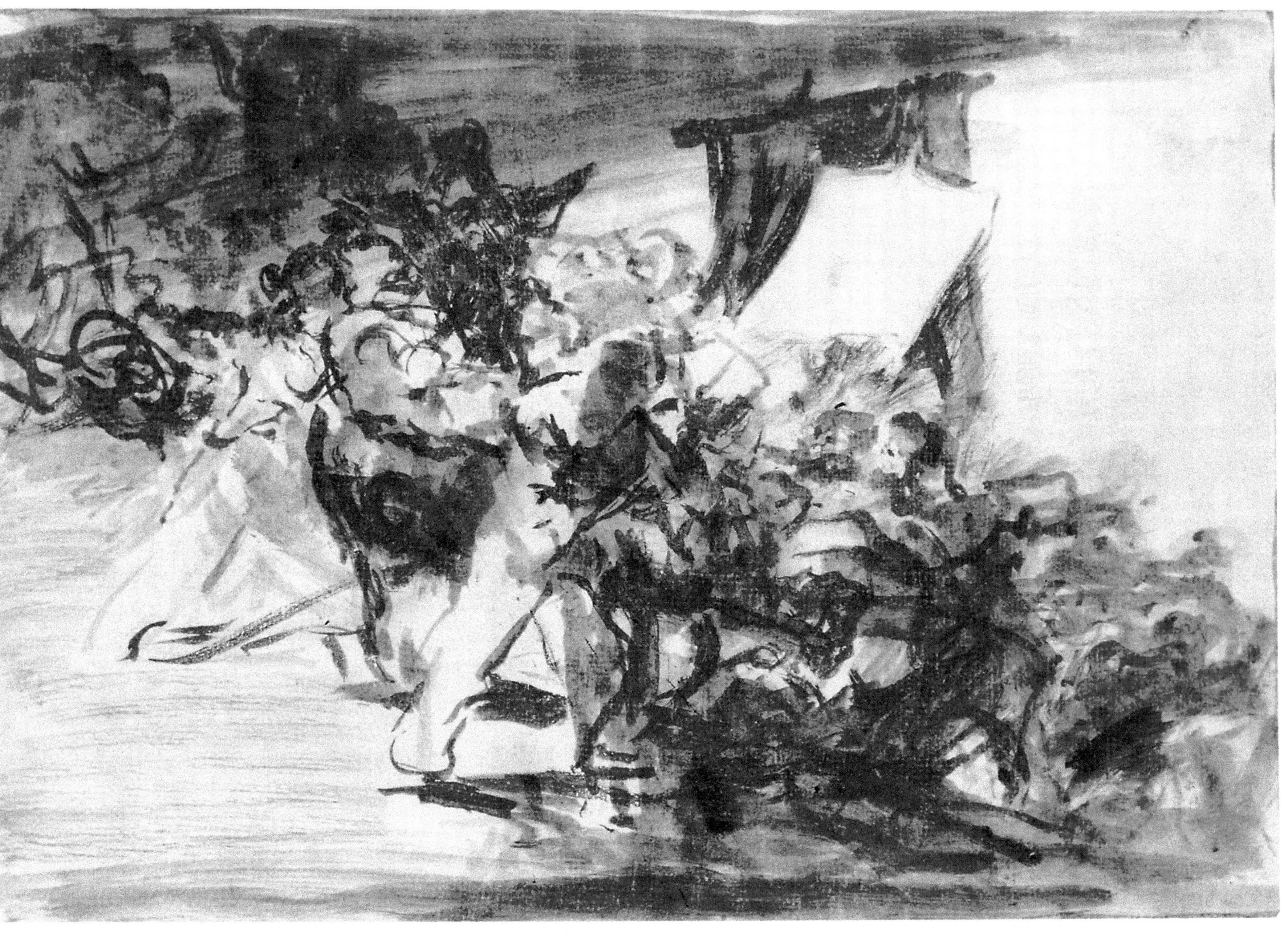

Unpublished preliminary drawing for a *Disparates* subject (from the collection of Mr. Philip Hofer)

GREAT GOYA ETCHINGS

THE PROVERBS, THE TAUROMAQUIA AND THE BULLS OF BORDEAUX

FRANCISCO GOYA

Introductions by
PHILIP HOFER

DOVER PUBLICATIONS
Garden City, New York

This Dover edition, first published in 2006, is a republication of all the illustrations from *The Disparates, or The Proverbios,* and *La Tauromaquia and The Bulls of Bordeaux,* both of which were first published by Dover Publications, New York, in 1969. The present edition also includes introductions by Philip Hofer, written specially for the 1969 volumes.

The 1969 editions contain reproductions of the following material (all courtesy of the owner, Mr. Philip Hofer, unless otherwise specified):

The unabridged first edition of Goya's *Disparates* (published in Madrid, 1864, by the Real Academia de Nobles Artes de San Fernando, under the title *Los Proverbios*), consisting of eighteen original etchings.

Rare pre-first-edition proofs of Nos. 12, 13 and 15.

Early states of the four *Disparates* etchings (Nos. 19–22) first published in 1877 by the magazine *L'Art* in Paris.

A preliminary drawing for a *Disparates* subject (first publication).

The unabridged first edition (1816) of the thirty-three basic plates of *La Tauromaquia,* and the first edition of the seven supplementary plates originally published by E. Loizelet, Paris, in 1876.

Three additional plates prepared for the *Tauromaquia* but not published by Goya ("The Daring of Martincho" courtesy of the Albertina, Vienna; the others courtesy of the Gabinete de Estampas, Biblioteca Nacional, Madrid).

A preliminary drawing for a *Tauromaquia* subject.

For purposes of comparison, two plates from Philip Hofer's Pepe Illo *Tauromaquia* of 1804.

Early impressions of the four basic lithographs of *The Bulls of Bordeaux (Los Toros de Burdeos)* series (in the collection of Philip Hofer) and a reproduction of the unique proof of a fifth, related lithograph (courtesy of the Musée des Beaux-Arts, Bordeaux).

Library of Congress Cataloging-in-Publication Data

Goya, Francisco, 1746–1828.
Great Goya etchings : the Proverbs, the Tauromaquia, and the Bulls of Bordeaux / Francisco Goya ; introductions by Philip Hofer.
p. cm.
Originally published: 1969.
ISBN-13: 978-0-486-44758-2
ISBN-10: 0-486-44758-8 (pbk.)
1. Goya, Francisco, 1746–1828. Proverbs. 2. Goya, Francisco, 1746–1828. Tauromaquia. 3. Goya, Francisco, 1746–1828. Bulls of Bordeaux. I. Hofer, Philip, 1898– II. Title.

NE2062.5.G6A4 2006
769.92—dc22

2005055594

Printed in Canada
44758809 2025
www.doverpublications.com

The Disparates
or, The Proverbios

Introduction to The Disparates or, The Proverbios

THE LAST OF Goya's four main print series, most often called by the public *Los Proverbios* (Proverbs), but also called by art historians, who have devised various names, *Los Disparates* (Follies—"without rhyme or reason") and even sometimes *Los Sueños* (Dreams), is the least known graphic work of the master, and the most difficult to appreciate or to understand. It is generally considered that Goya made the eighteen large etchings and aquatints that the series, as first officially published in 1864, contains soon after a particularly serious illness he underwent in 1819. He had just moved into a newly purchased house on the banks of the Manzanares, north of Madrid—a house which became locally known as "La Quinta del Sordo" (the house of the deaf man). For Goya was nearly totally deaf, and was seventy-three years old. His wife had died in 1811; his only son, Francisco Javier, was an idler and of little help to him; his popularity at court and among those who commissioned pictures was at a low ebb; Spain itself staggered along under the stupid and autocratic rule of one of the worst of its Bourbon kings, Ferdinand VII. Small wonder, then, that Goya was deeply discouraged and recovered from his illness with the greatest difficulty. There was little in his life, or in its prospects, to give him hope. This print series surely reflects his state of mind.

One cannot be sure what name Goya himself had intended for the prints under consideration. Perhaps *Disparates* is the most likely one, since a certain very limited number of proof prints, drawn from the plates by the artist himself, carry this title in a contemporary handwriting (two are reproduced in this volume). Moreover, the full title of each print was, as usual, disguised in order that its personal, political, religious, or satirical inspiration could not be identified. Why should a group of dark human figures huddled together on the branch of a great tree be called "Disparate ridículo" (Ridiculous folly) if a meaning was to be inferred therefrom? Like the terrifying murals Goya painted in his house about the same time, called popularly *las pinturas negras* (the black paintings), this subject seems almost a vision from a nightmare. We know that Goya was deeply disturbed nervously as well as physically after a previous illness in 1792–94, and that he turned to making prints *before* he had gained sufficient strength to resume painting and his normal life. It may have been that the same sequence of suffering and work occurred in 1819–20. But whereas many of the *Caprichos* (Caprices) series etched and aquatinted in the late 1790's are susceptible to reasonable interpretation, the same is not true of the *Disparates* series. As the eminent Spanish Goya scholar F. J. Sánchez Cantón says, how can we explain them rationally when we can hardly find words with which to describe them?

Besides the eighteen *Disparates* prints that the Academia de San Fernando in Madrid published in 1864, thirty-six years after Goya's death, there are four more prints of equal size and of the same enigmatic purport which were first published in the French magazine *L'Art* in Paris in 1877. These seem also to have been intended by Goya to form part of this series. This makes a total of twenty-two subjects. Can we carry any of these compositions back into the stage of drawings which Goya customarily made while he was working out the subjects of the prints? Actually we can; but the relation to the prints is more than usually involved. There are nineteen drawings recorded for subjects which are in the *Disparates* vein and of similar size and technique. Eighteen of these are in the Prado Museum in Madrid, and one is in the possession of the author of this essay. The latter drawing appears as the frontispiece of this volume, where it is reproduced for the first time. It is not difficult to relate thirteen of these drawings to the same number of *Disparates* prints. But there are six drawings for which no prints are known to exist, and nine prints (Löys Delteil nos. 206, 209, 214, 215, 219, 220, 221, 222, and 223) for which there seem to be no drawings. None of the four prints first published in *L'Art* seem to have preliminary drawings, but they are nevertheless unmistakably by the master.

It has been tempting in recent times for psychologists and psychiatrists to try to analyze Goya's state of mind which produced the *Disparates* prints and the *pinturas negras,* but so far no considerable group of Goya scholars has seemed satisfied with any single interpretation. It is one thing to hazard a guess, and quite another thing to attempt to *interpret* the mind of a man who died one hundred and forty years ago. In the end it would seem best to look at these prints without trying to discover any very specific meaning—to loosen one's aesthetic emotions and to allow one's unfettered imagination to revel in or be stirred by the train of thoughts and emotions the prints evoke.

Dover Publications is doing a public service in making good reproductions of the *Disparates* prints available. All of the many editions of the series put out by the Academia de San Fernando have become scarce. A privately printed edition of the first eighteen subjects, said to have been prepared for "a Madrid industrialist" who temporarily owned the original copper plates before the Academia (ca. 1840–50), is almost as rare as the proof prints, but it has pale impressions of the prints (one of the best—*Disparate* 13—is reproduced in this book). The first published edition of 1864 was therefore the basic one used here, together with the two above-mentioned proofs pulled by Goya himself (for *Disparates* 12 and 15). These are all strong and contain added aquatint grain. If the reproductions in this volume naturally cannot be as fine as the originals from which they were made, they are at least better than the worn ghosts of impressions that have recently come from the heavily used and reworked plates.

Cambridge, Massachusetts
October 1968

PHILIP HOFER
Harvard Library

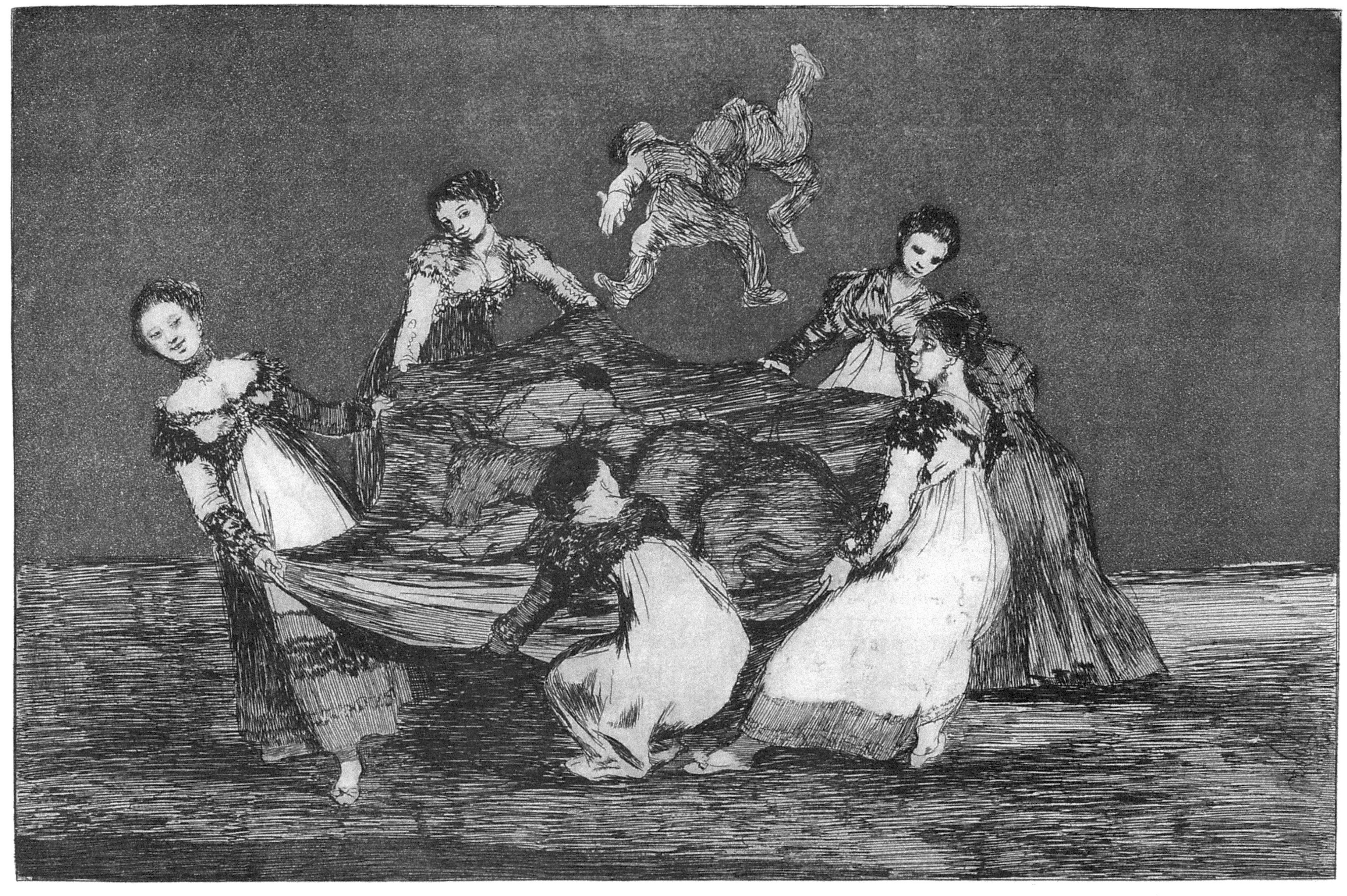

1 DISPARATE FEMENINO / *Feminine folly*

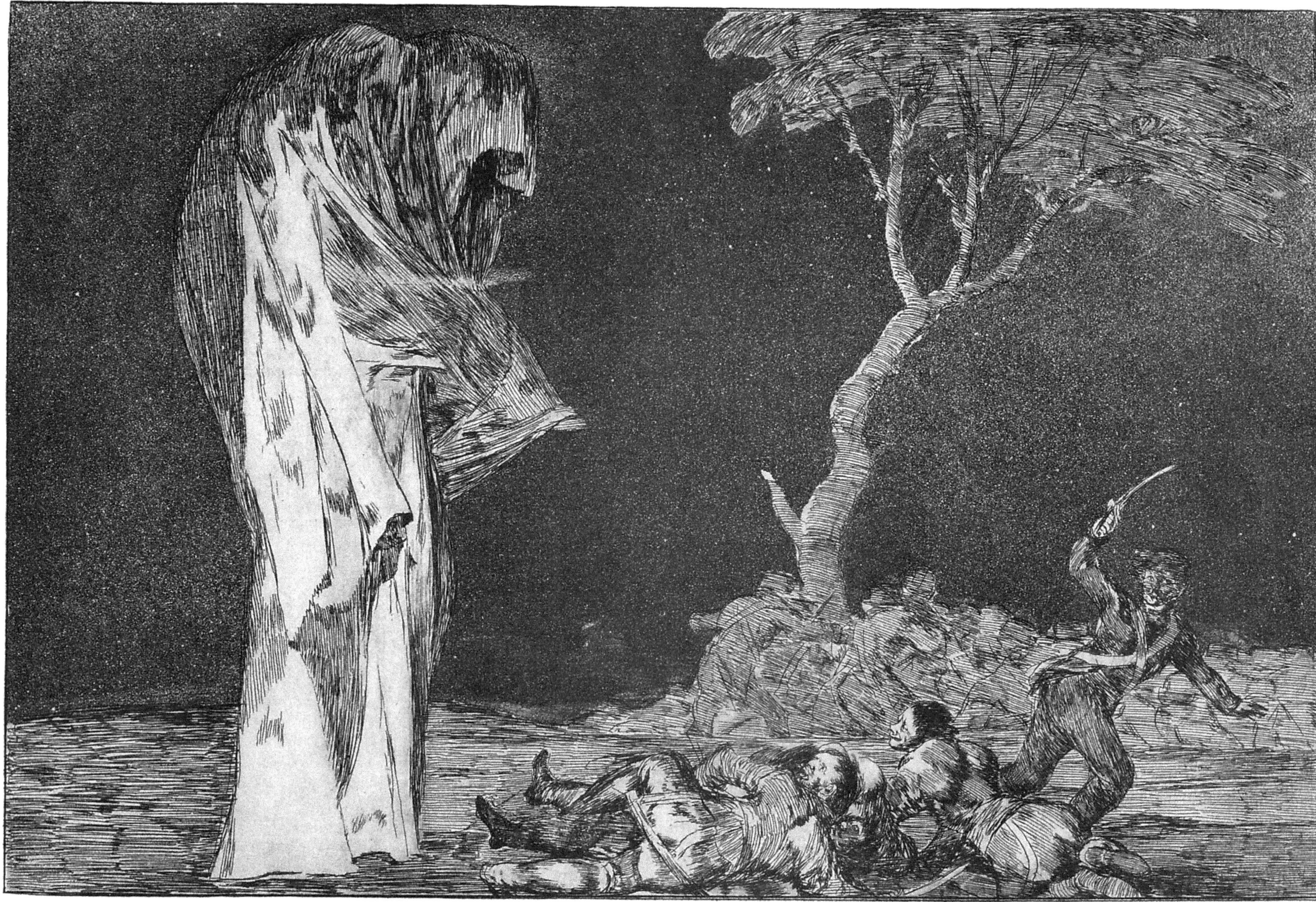

2 Disparate de miedo / *Folly of fear*

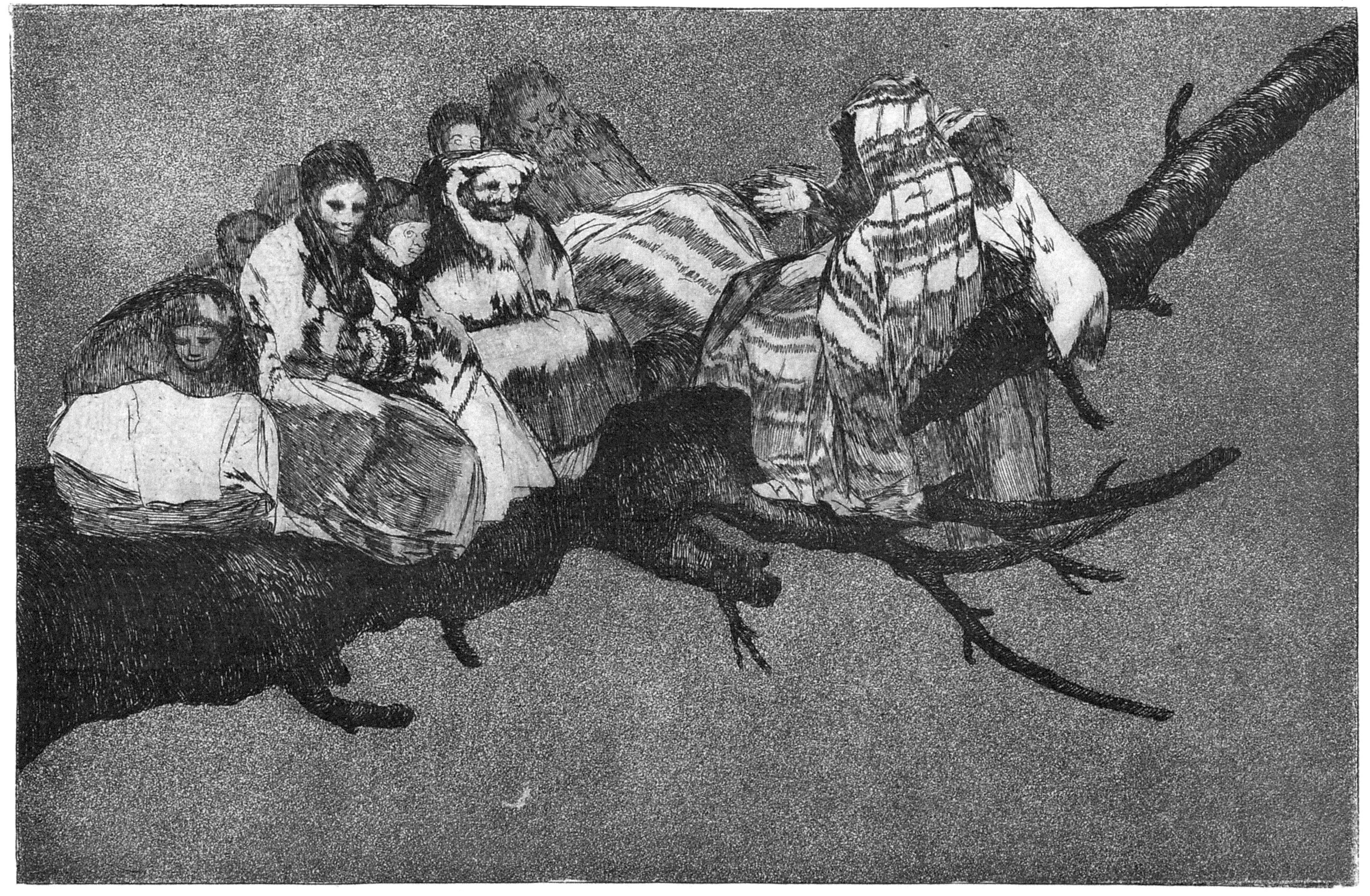

3 Disparate ridículo / *Ridiculous folly*

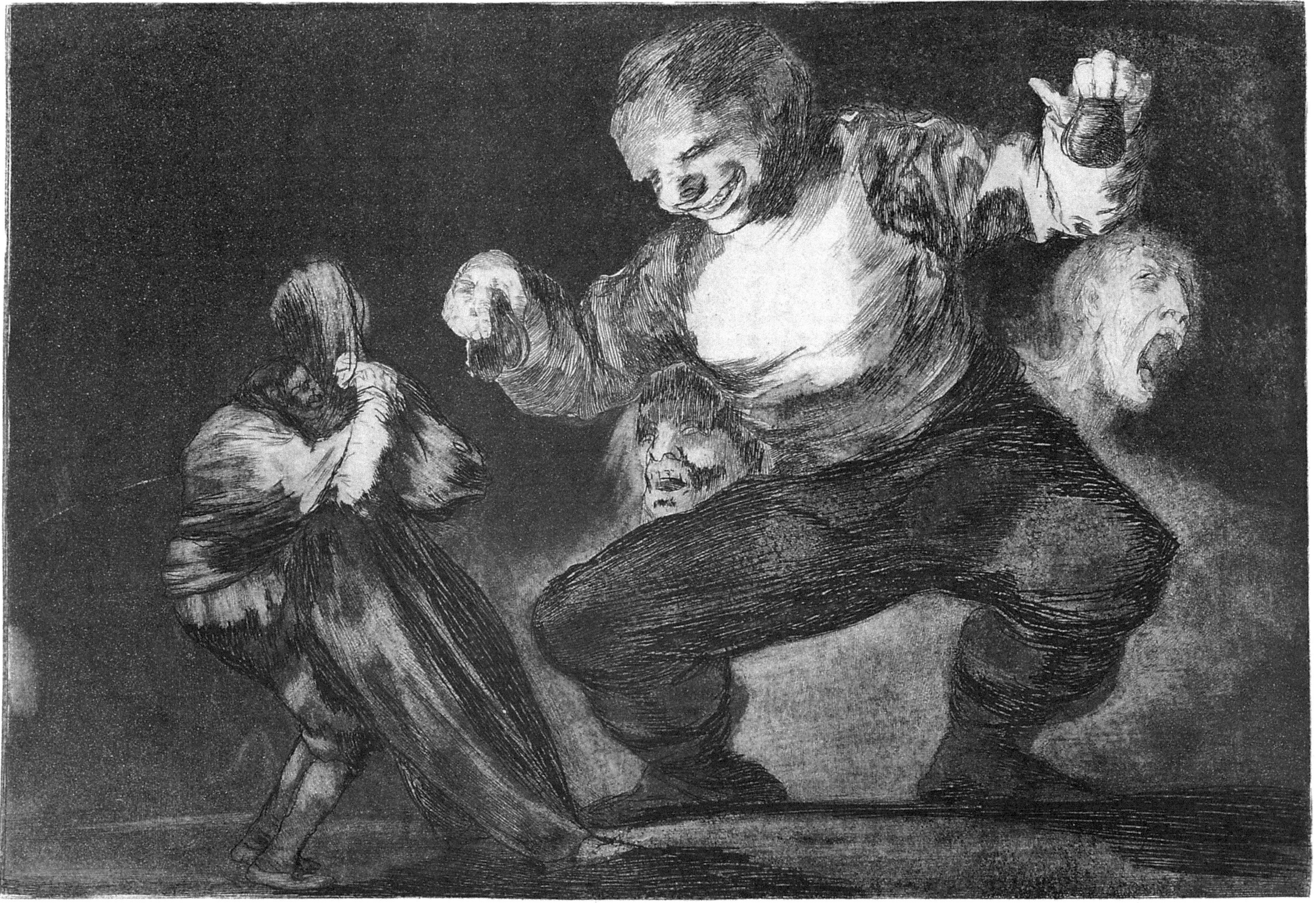

4 Bobalicón / *Big booby*

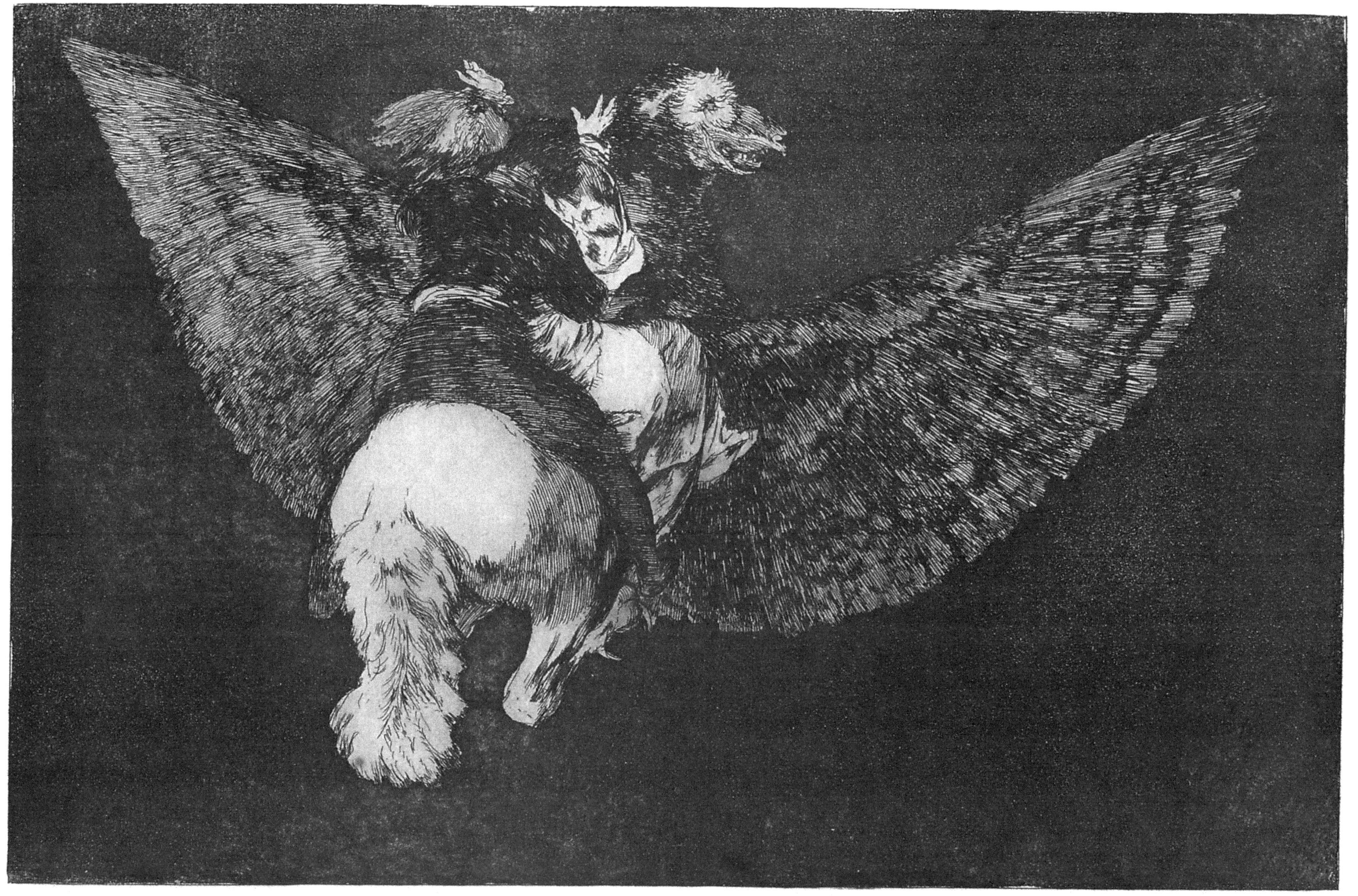

5 DISPARATE VOLANTE / *Flying folly*

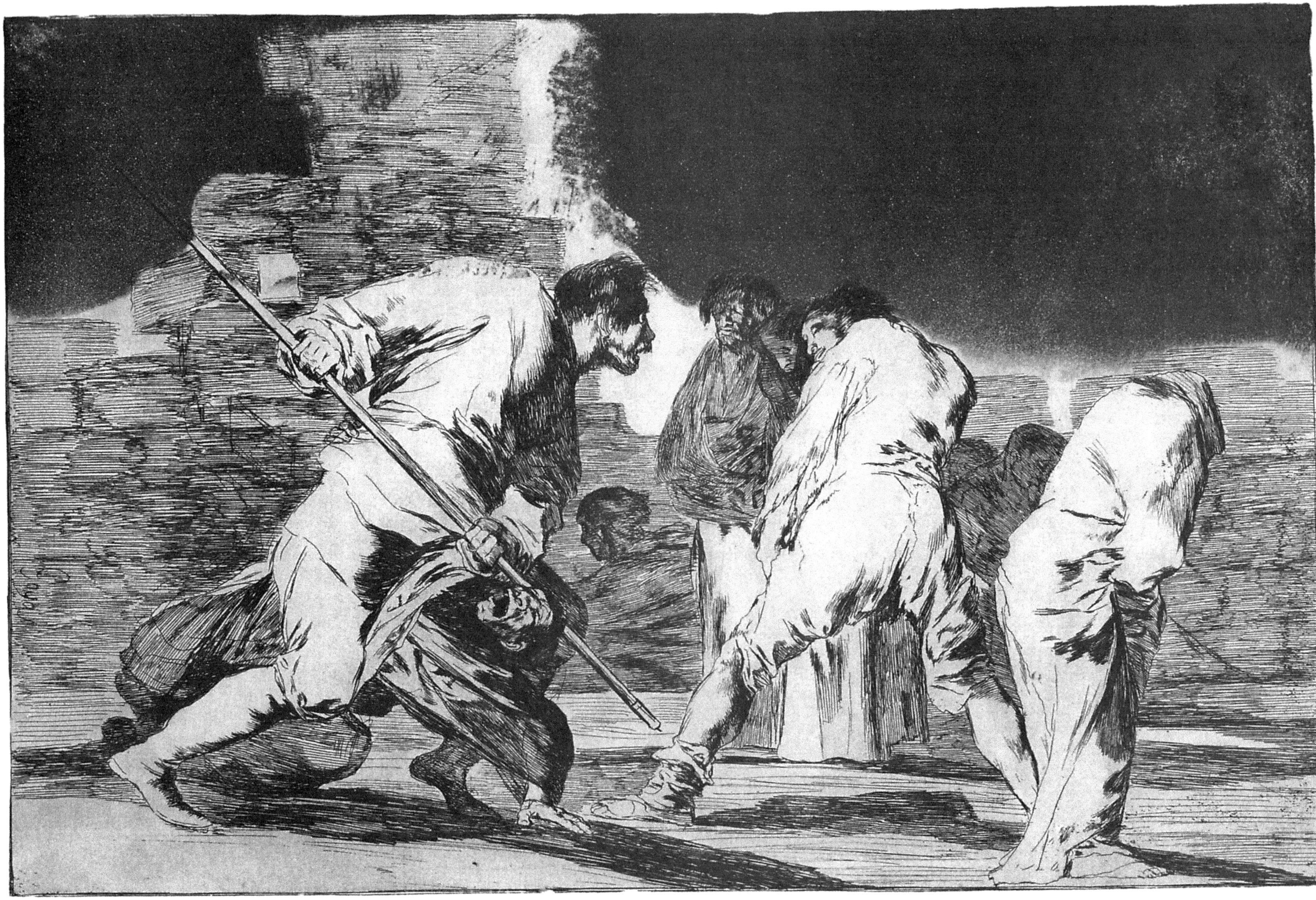

6 Disparate furioso / *Furious folly*

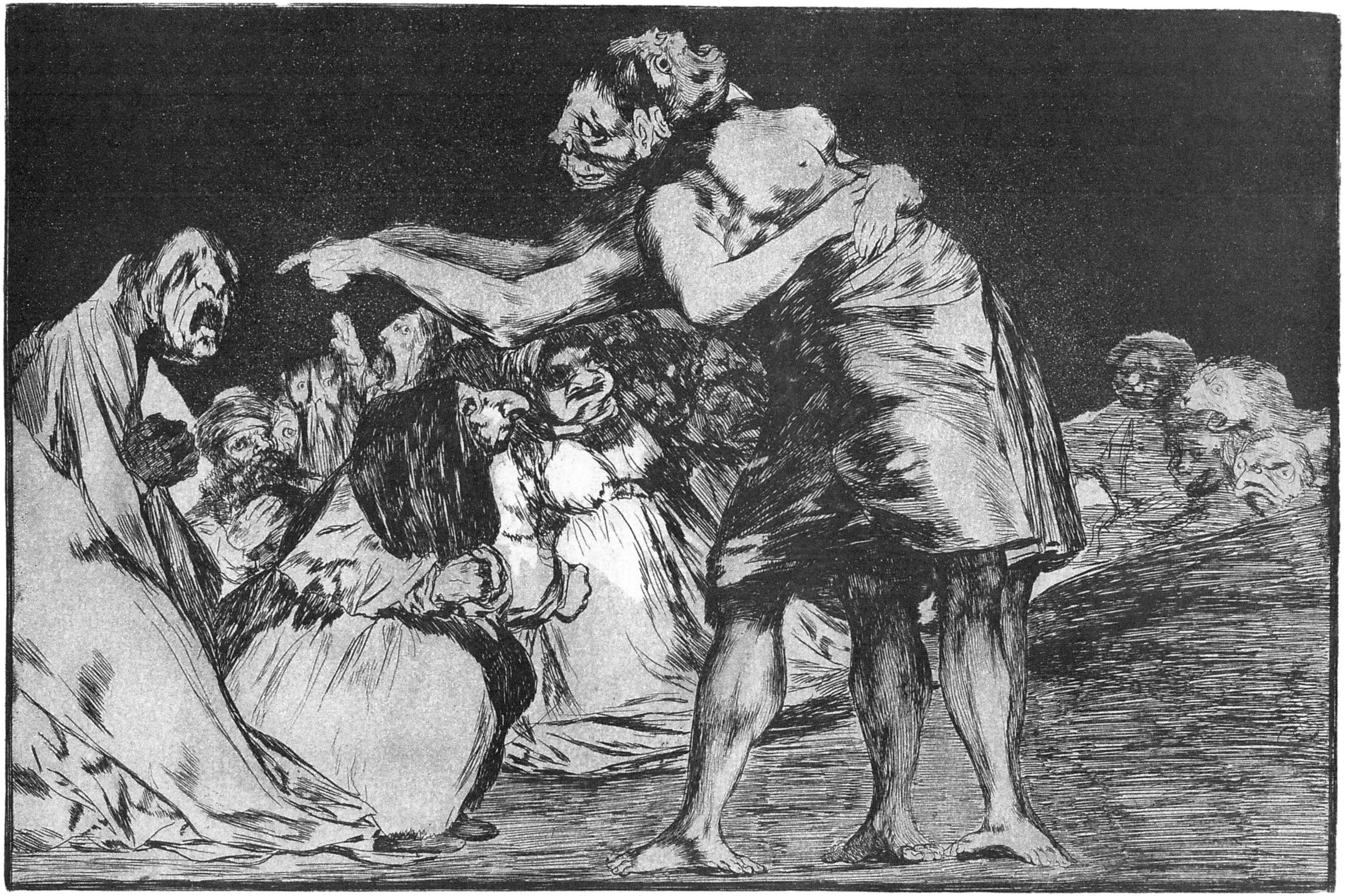

7 Disparate desordenado [Disparate matrimonial] / *Disordered folly [Matrimonial folly]*

8 Los ensacados / *The men in sacks*

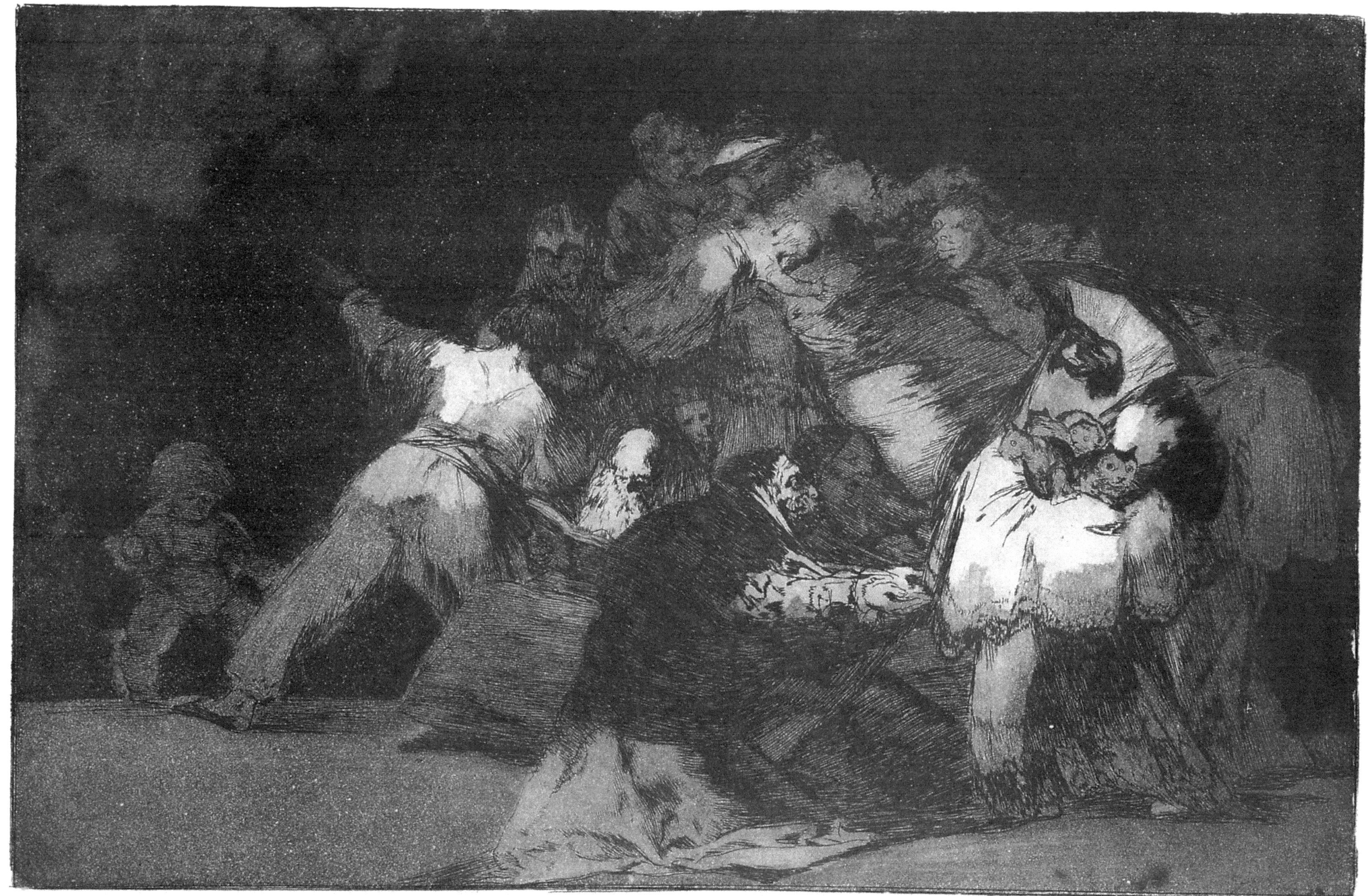

9 Disparate general / *General folly*

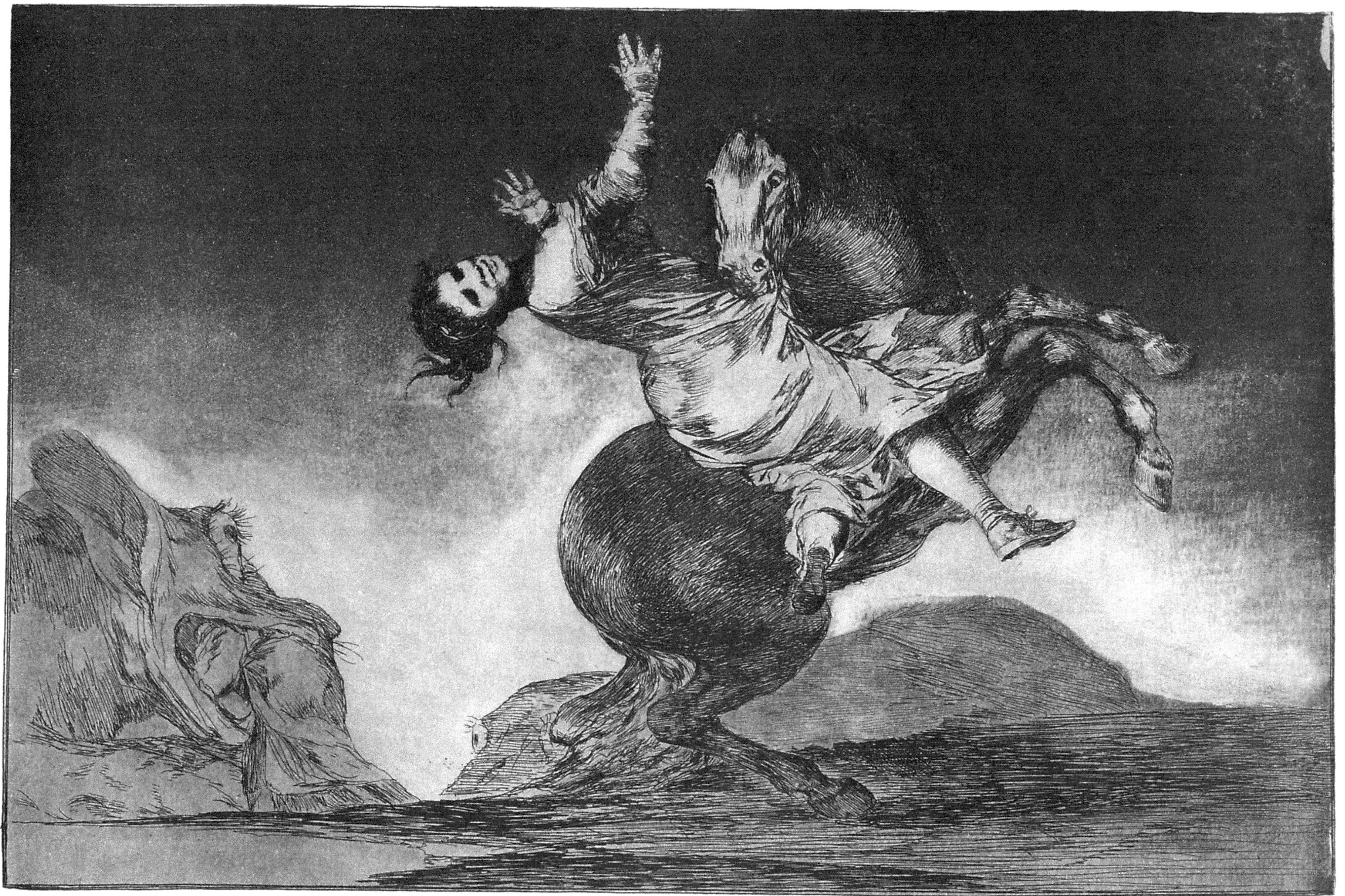

10 El caballo raptor / *The kidnapping horse*

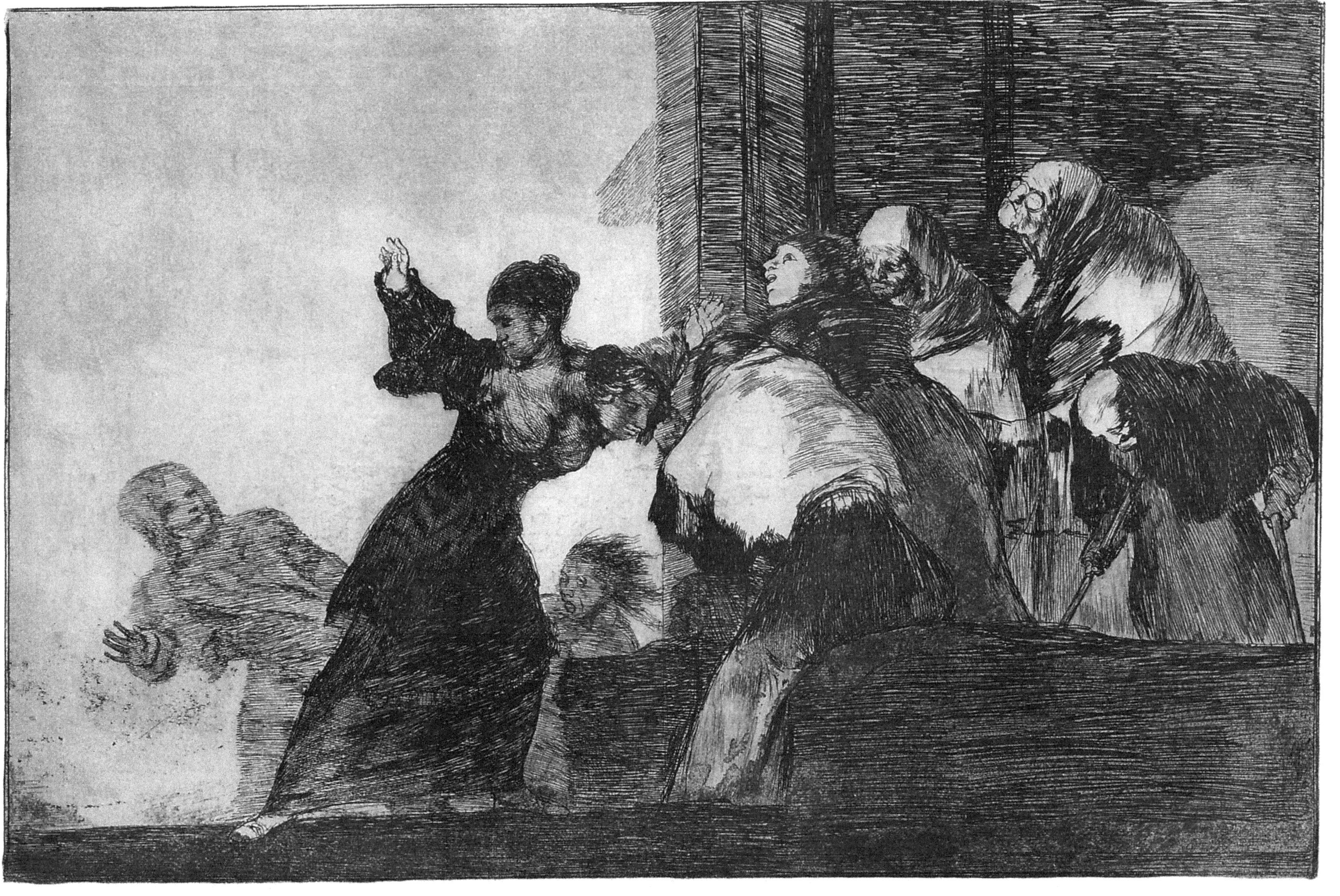

11 Disparate pobre / *Poor folly*

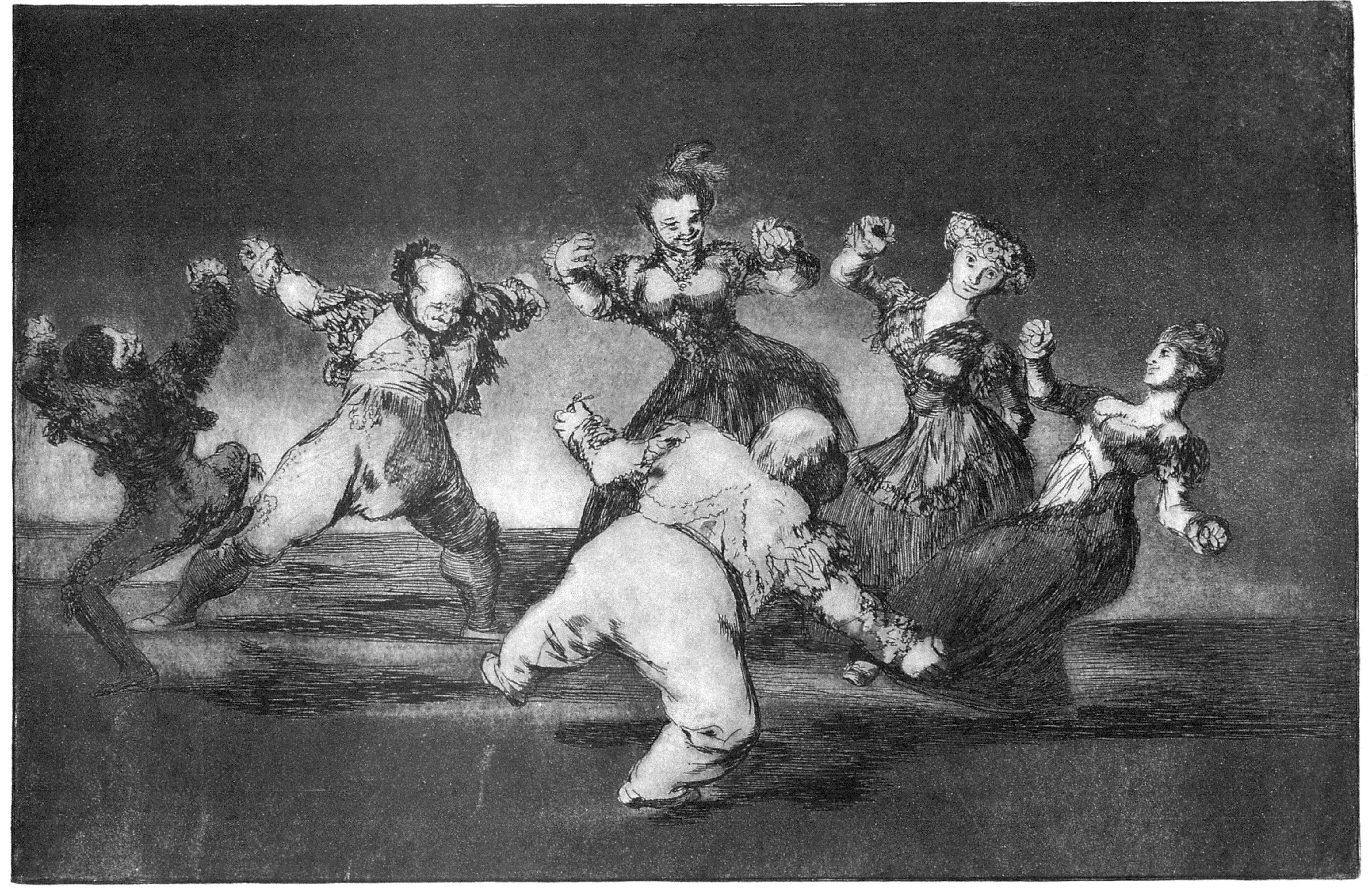

12 DISPARATE ALEGRE / *Merry folly*

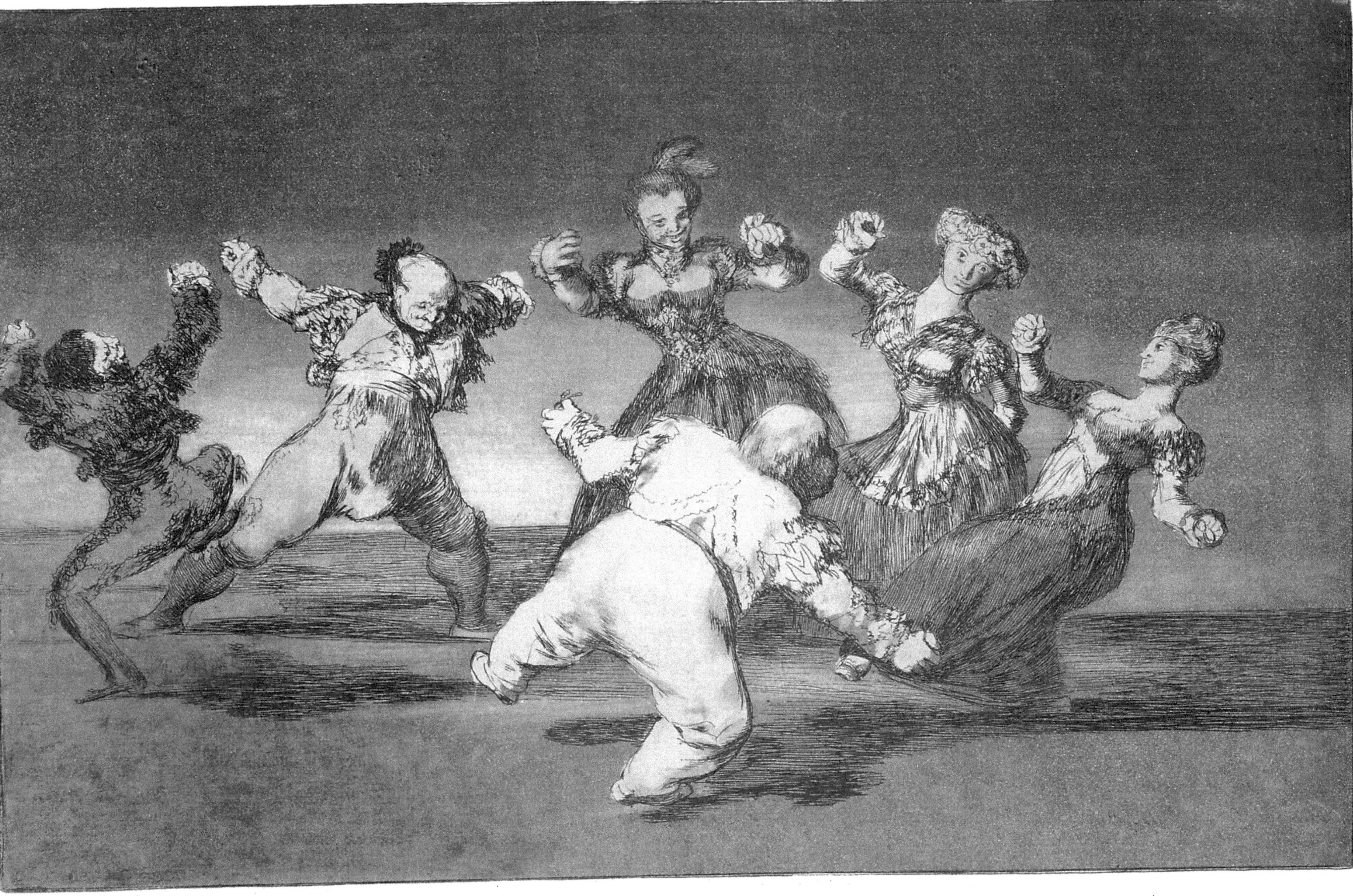

12A Artist's working proof of No. 12 [Disparate alegre]

13 MODO DE VOLAR / *Way of flying*

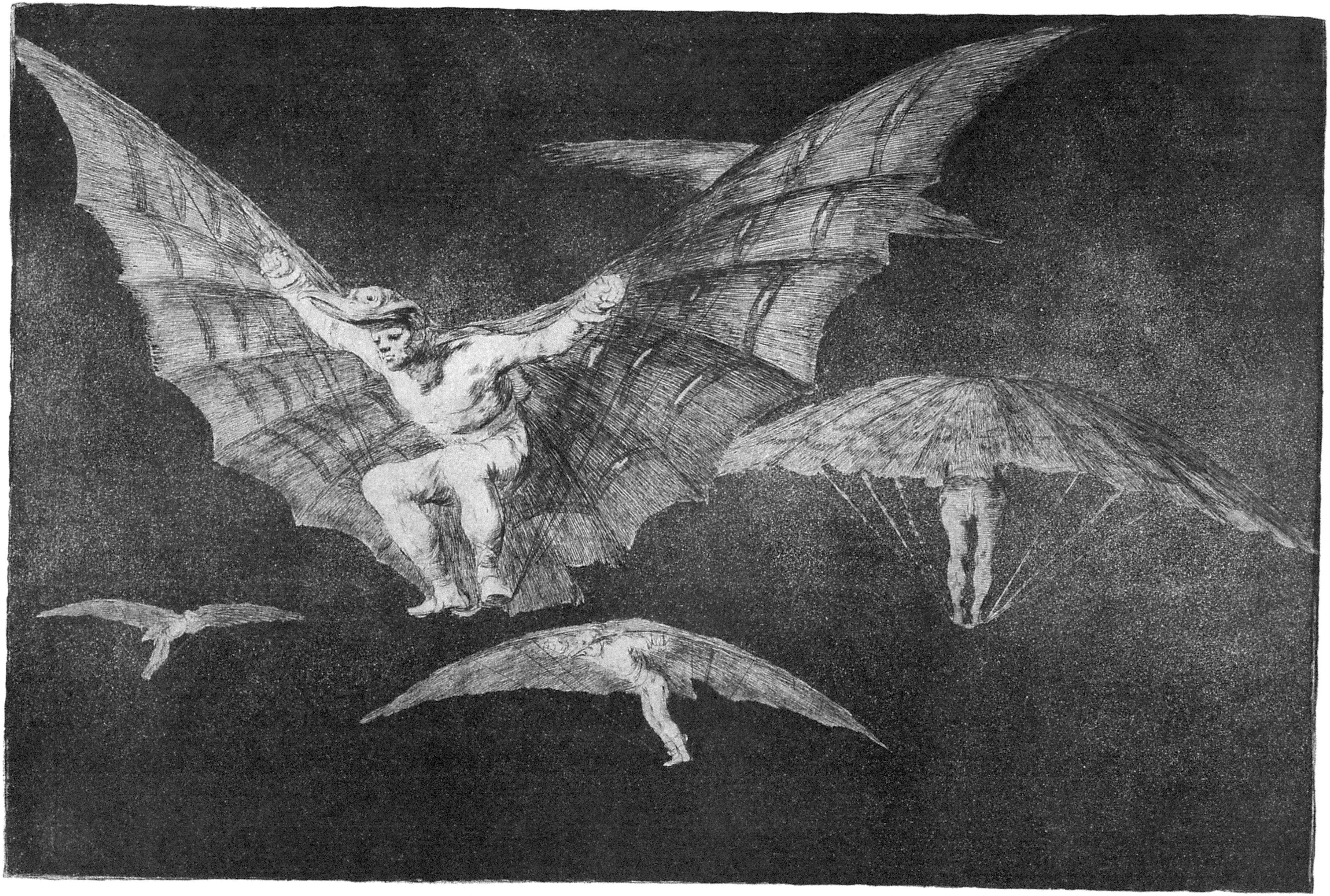

13A Proof of No. 13 [Modo de volar] pulled ca. 1840–50

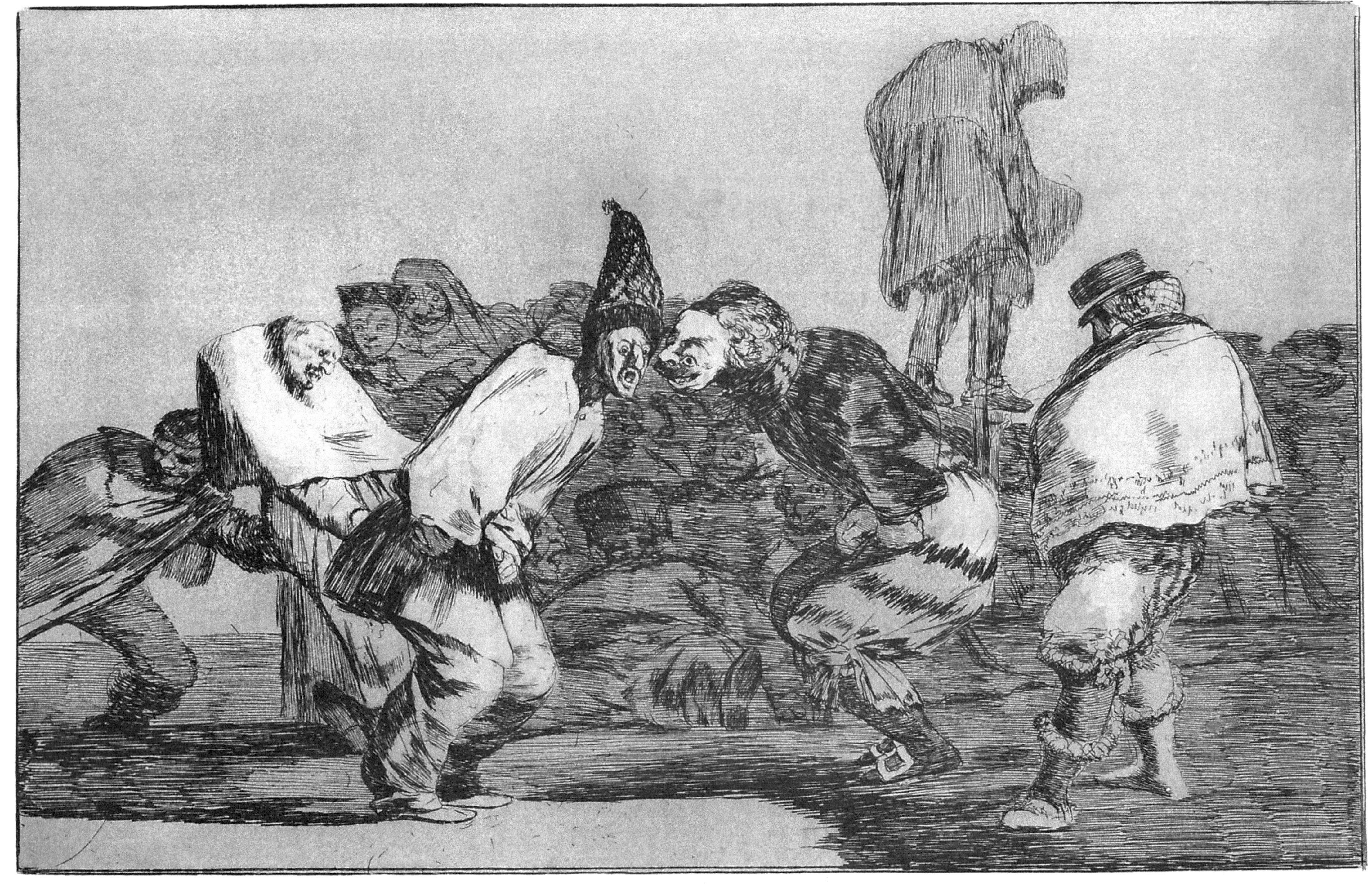

14 Disparate de carnaval / *Carnival folly*

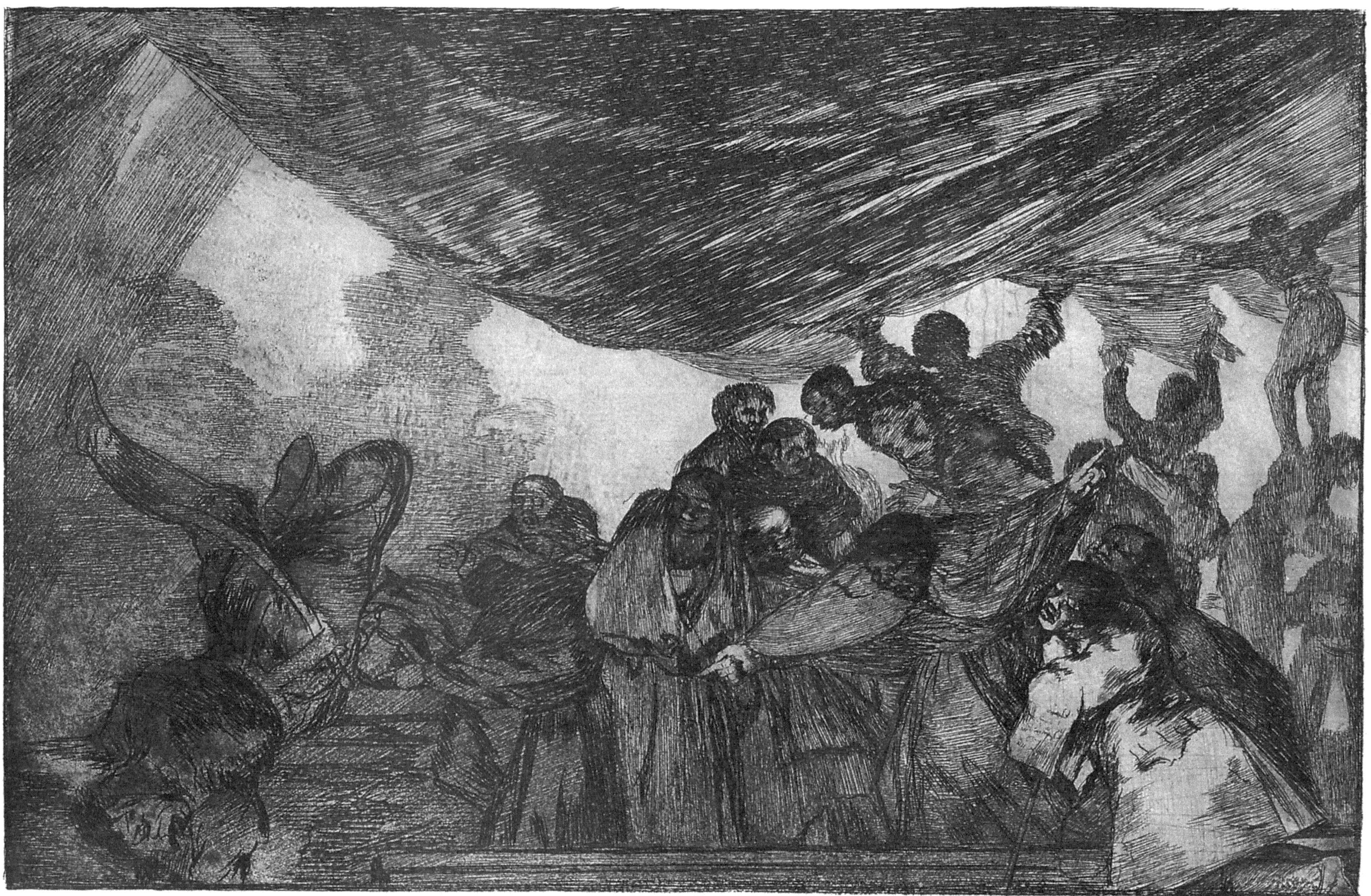

15 Disparate claro / *Clear folly*

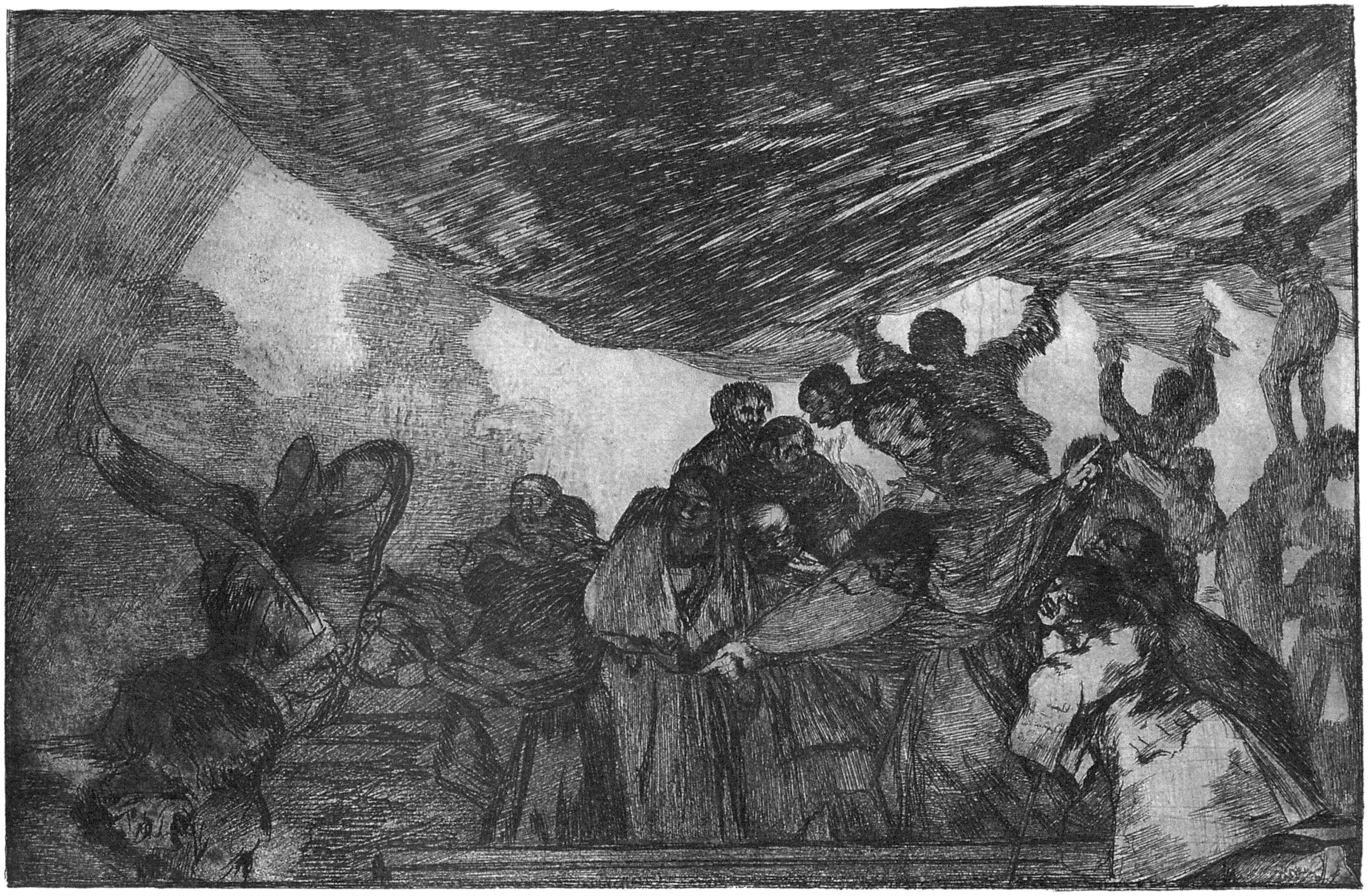

15 Disparate claro / *Clear folly*

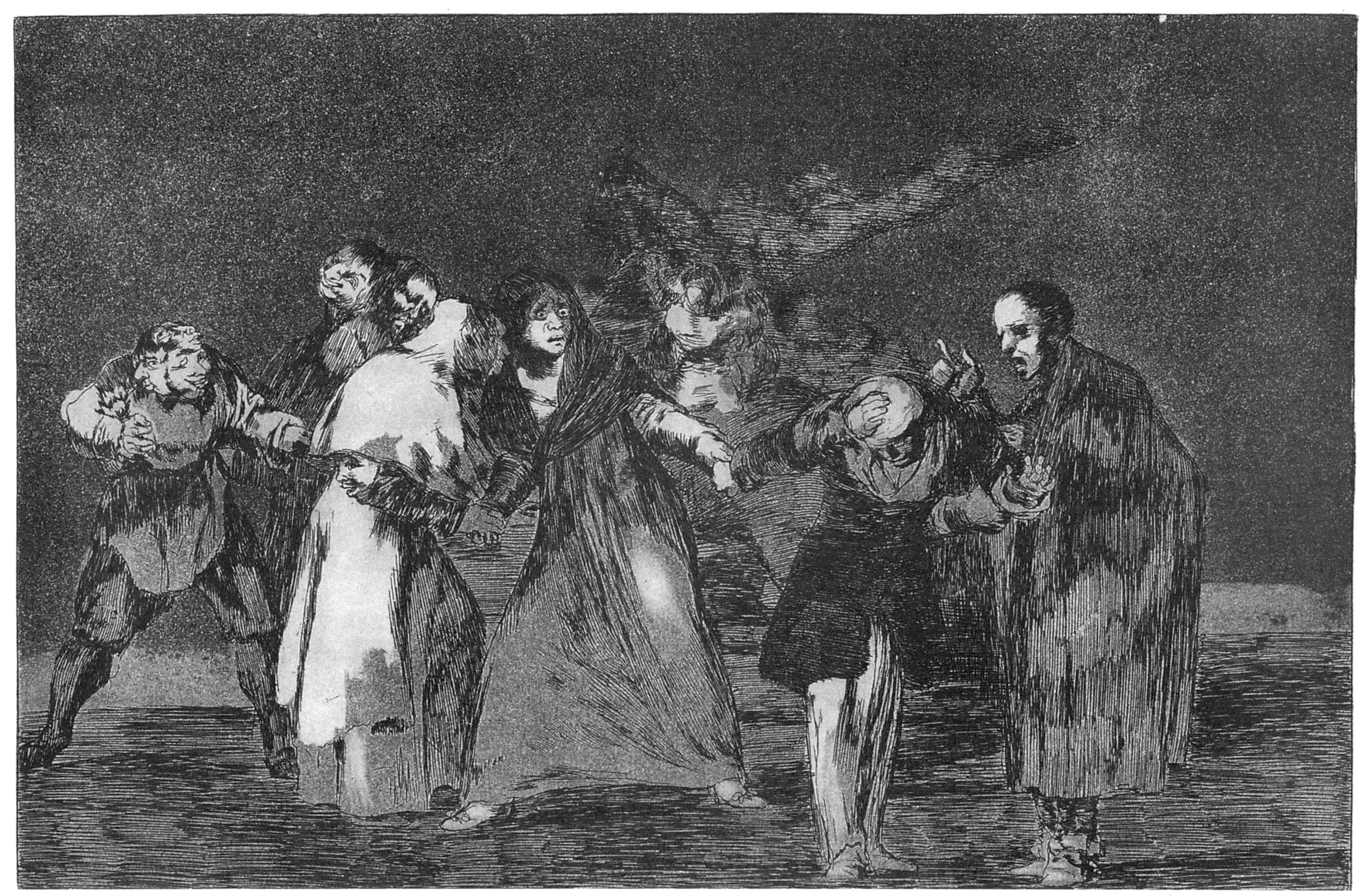

16 Untitled

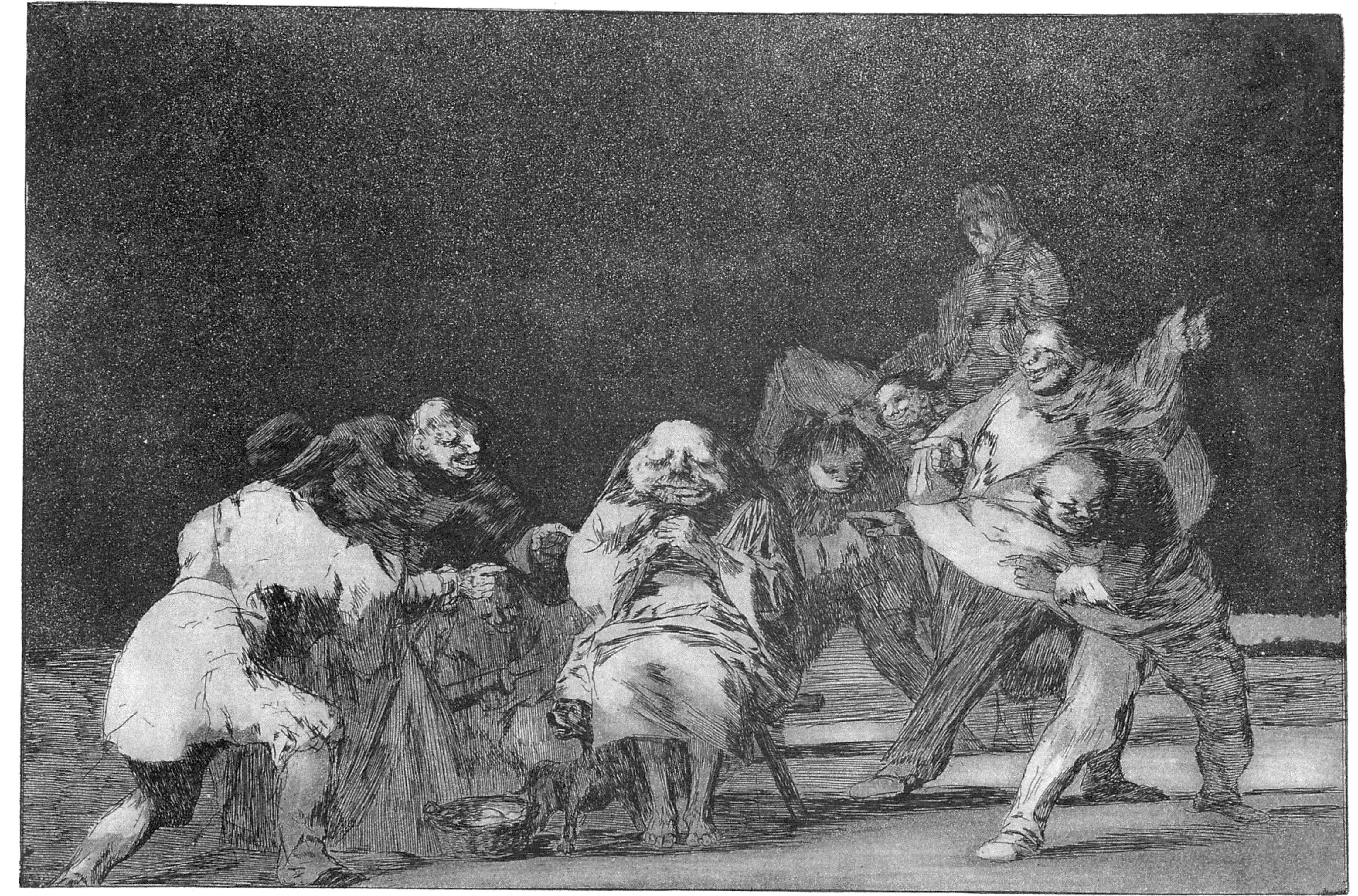

17 La lealtad / *Loyalty*

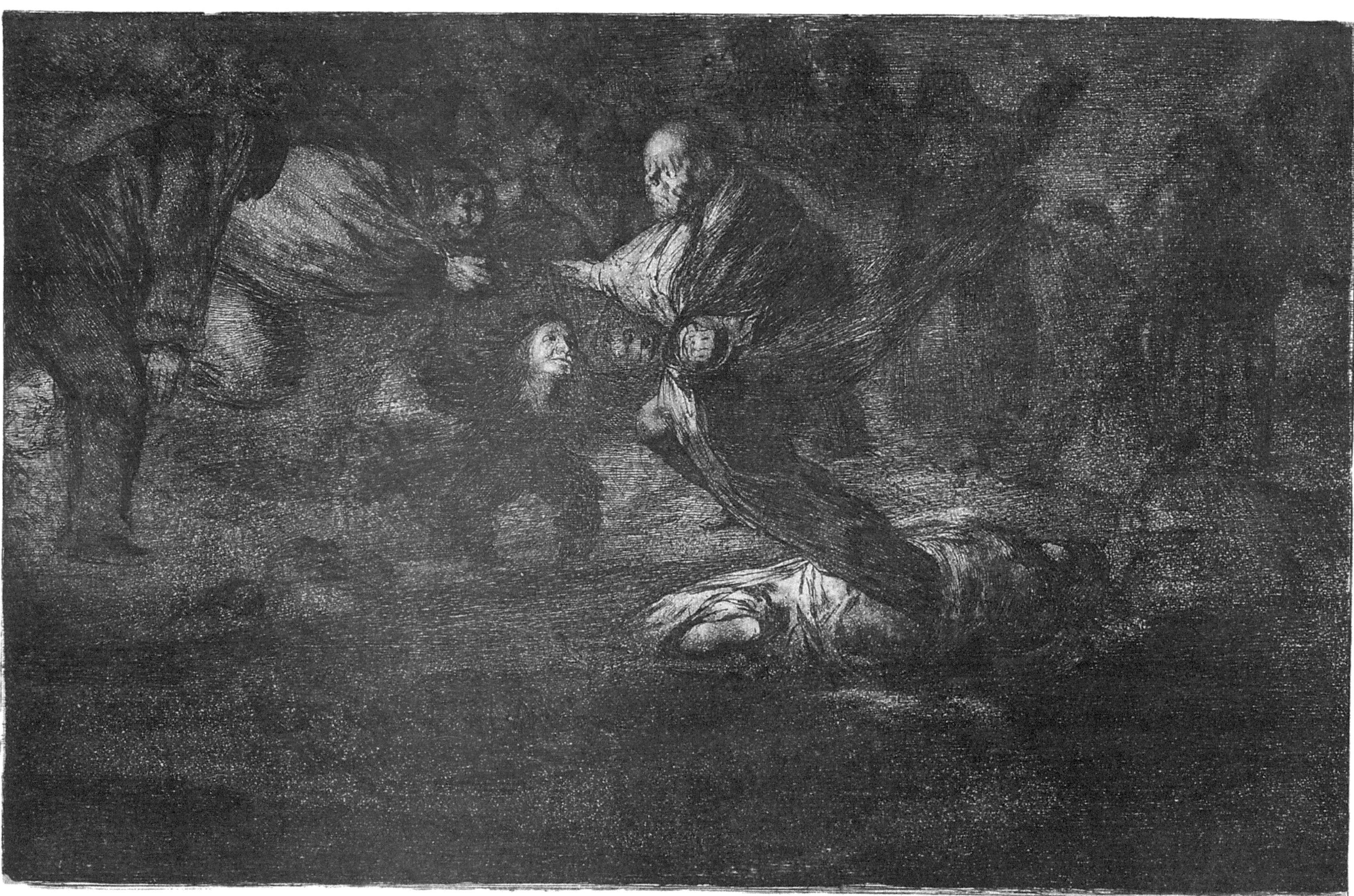

18 Untitled

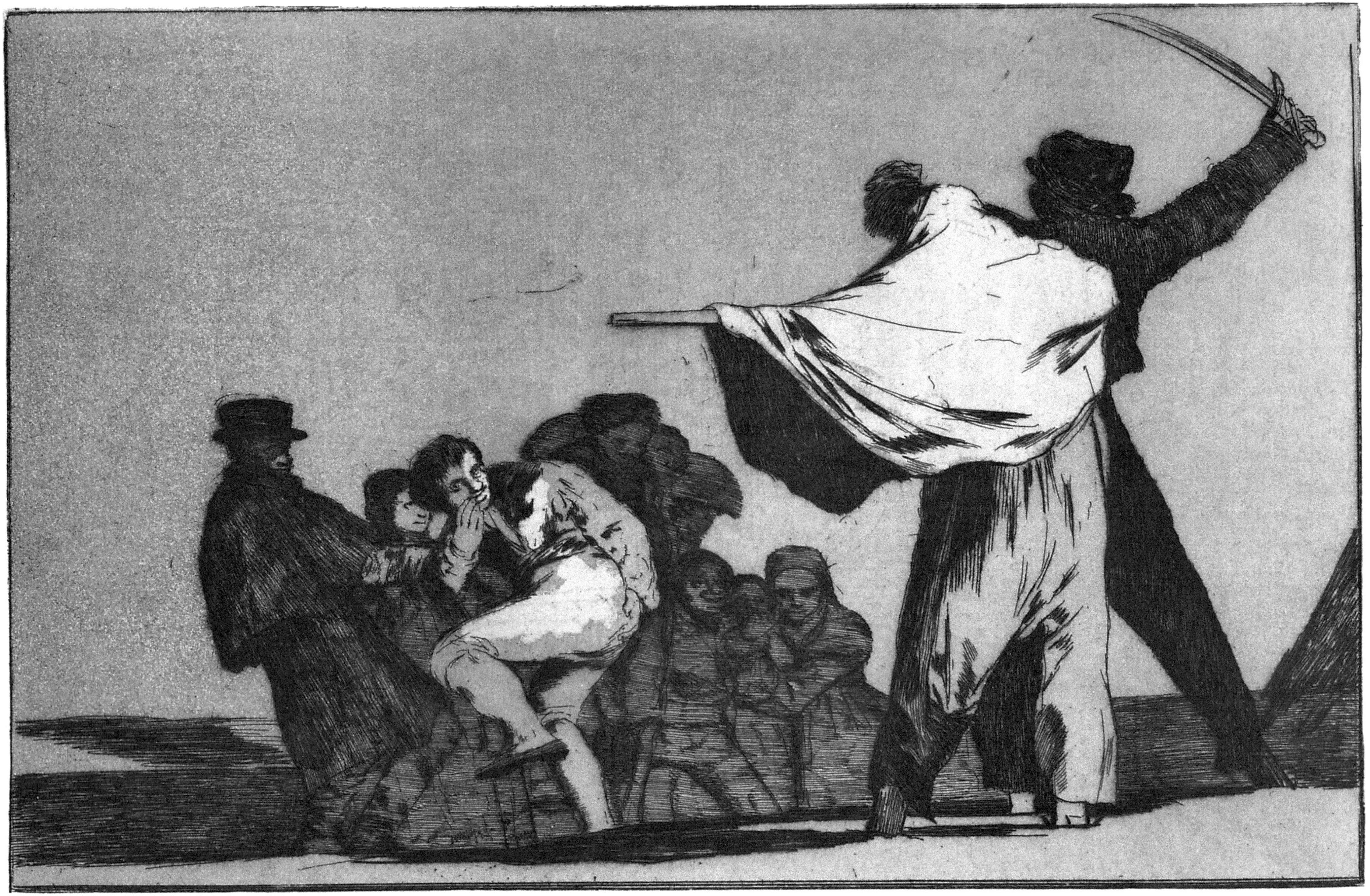

19 Disparate conocido [¡Qué guerrero!] / *Well-known folly* [*What a warrior!*]

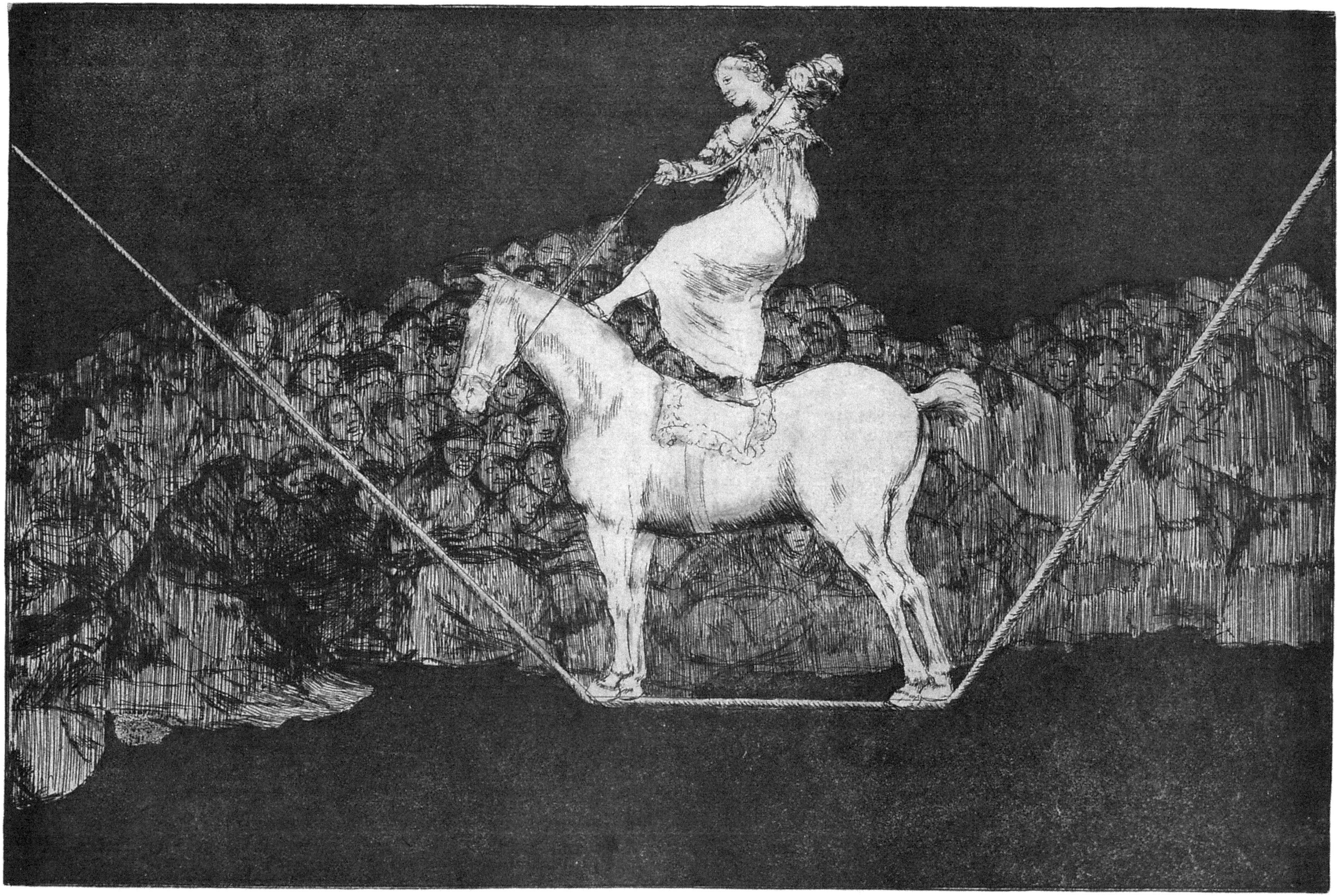

20 Disparate puntual [Una reina del circo] / *Punctual folly* [*A circus queen*]

21 Disparate de bestia [Otras leyes por el pueblo] / *Animal folly* [*Other laws for the people*]

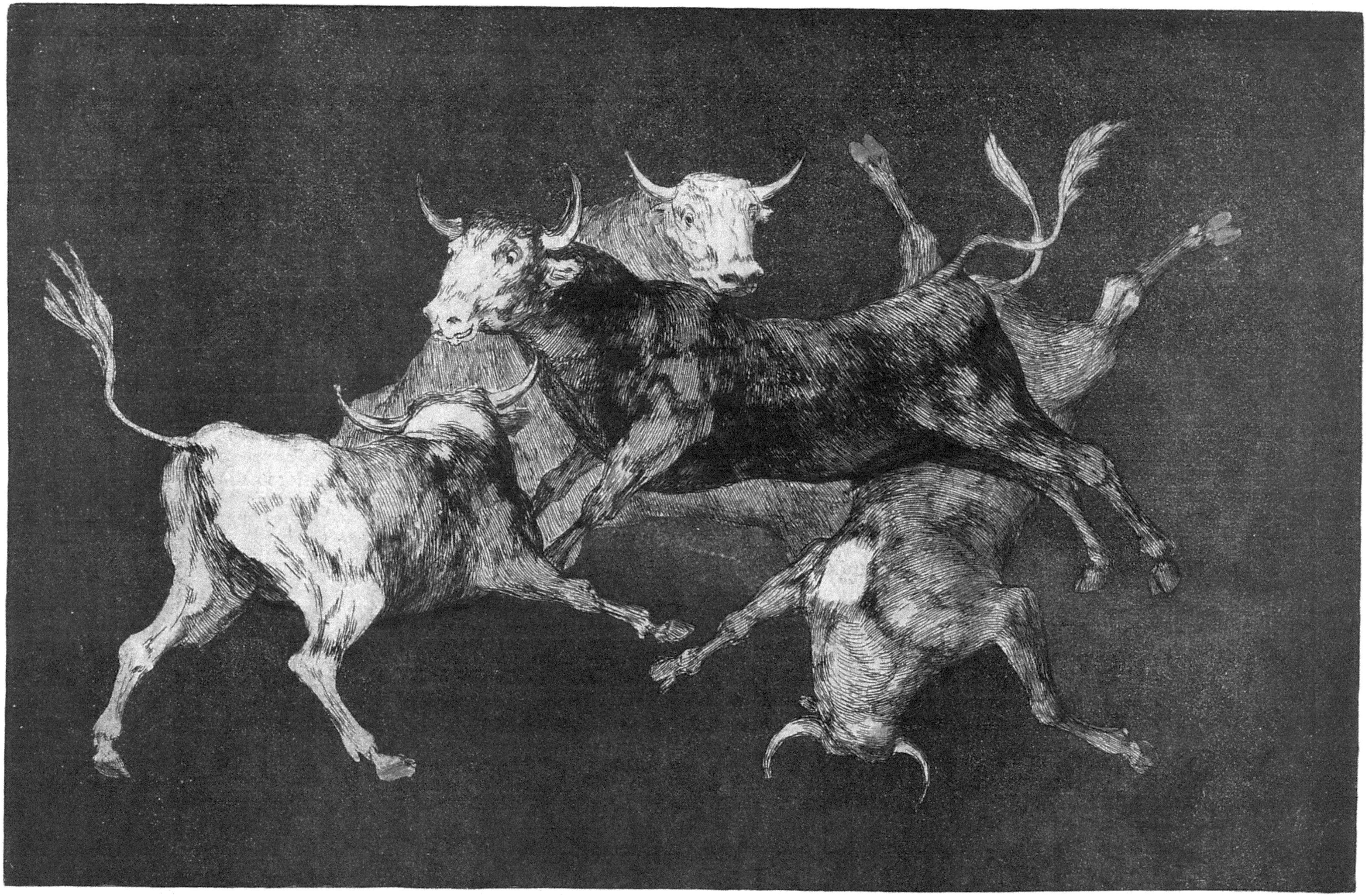

22 Disparate de toritos [Lluvia de toros] / *Folly of young bulls* [*Rain of bulls*]

La Tauromaquia

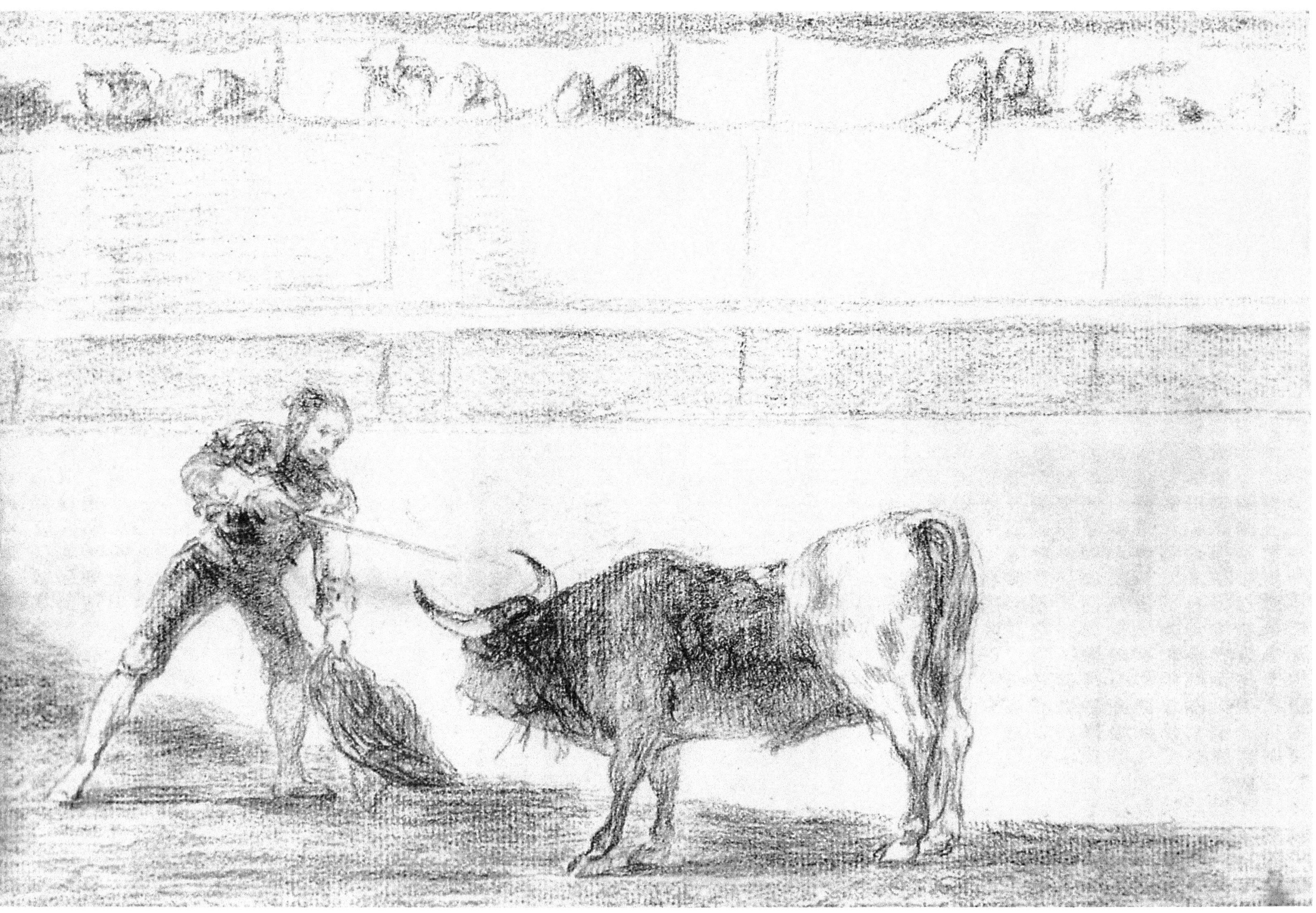

Preliminary drawing for Plate 30 of the *Tauromaquia* . . .

Introduction to La Tauromaquia

OF GOYA'S FOUR major print series, only two were issued publicly in the artist's lifetime: the *Caprichos* (Caprices) and the *Tauromaquia* (Bullfights). The exact publication dates of both are known, thanks to a newspaper called the *Diario de Madrid.* It was February 6, 1799 for the first named series, and October 28, 1816 for this later one. However it is unlikely that many copies were issued then in view of the recent end of the Spanish War of Liberation—although not because the plates were politically controversial as the *Caprichos* had been. Miss Eleanor Sayre of the Museum of Fine Arts, Boston, thinks that most of the so-called first edition was not even printed until Javier Goya, the artist's only son, obtained possession of the copper plates and ordered a considerable supply of impressions made after Goya died in 1828.

If the greatest of the early Goya collectors, Valentín Carderera, is correct, the artist began his plates during the very first years of the nineteenth century, even though the only date to be found on any of the prints is 1815. Enrique Lafuente Ferrari, an excellent Spanish scholar, has demonstrated that it was at first Goya's intention to illustrate a much enlarged edition of a rather unpretentious little book on bullfighting by Nicolás Fernández de Moratín, father of Goya's close personal friend, the playwright Leandro de Moratín. This small octavo had been published at Madrid without illustrations in 1777. And since Goya, by his own say so, had always been deeply interested in bullfighting (one must recall he even signed himself occasionally "Francisco de los Toros"), what could be more natural than that by 1801, when any more active rôle than observation was barred by his increasing and serious deafness, as well as by his age (fifty-five), he should seek an excuse to picture the subject? The prints on bullfighting current in Madrid at that time were poor, and the sport had become increasingly popular.

This writer does not think it has ever been noticed that by 1804, at least, Goya could have had a visual prototype before him with the very title of *Tauromaquia,* a book written by the famous bullfighter José Delgado, popularly called "Pepe Illo." Like Moratín's booklet, the first edition of this work, published at Cadiz in 1796, is not illustrated. But perhaps the second edition of 1801 was, and another edition of 1804 certainly is, for the writer possesses a copy of it. Here there are thirty simple, small (3 x 5-inch) engraved scenes from bullfights, oblong in form, with a number of compositional resemblances so close to Goya's thirty-three vastly improved and enlarged (9½ x 13½-inch) oblong plates that there almost surely was a connection. It was Goya's habit to seek inspiration from other prints; this was discovered by Miss Sayre in the case of the *Caprichos,* and is evident from the fact that Goya actually copied Velázquez. But after that first group of large engravings after Velázquez (made in 1778), Goya always elaborated on as well as outdid his visual sources. And he never succeeded better than in the case of his own *Tauromaquia,* which notably honors the small book's author "Pepe Illo," whom Goya personally knew, in the subjects and the actual printed titles of Plates 29 and 33. The latter is Goya's last subject in the first edition of 1816—"The unlucky death of Pepe Illo in the ring at Madrid"—a fitting and dramatic conclusion to his series.

On the 2nd of May, 1808, soon after Napoleon installed his brother Joseph Bonaparte on the Spanish throne with the aid of French troops, civil war broke out in Spain. Almost at once all peaceful projects were driven out of Goya's mind. His eighty prints of the *Desastres de la Guerra* (Disasters of War) must have been begun soon after this time. It is not supposed that he again took up the *Tauromaquia* theme, so suddenly interrupted, until the Peninsular War was ended by Wellington's victories of 1814. Certainly his Plates 19, 29 and 31 carry "1815" as well as the artist's name, and the French critic Paul Lefort says that trial proofs of no. 28 do also. Therefore, we guess that the last fourteen plates—nearly half the series—may be post-Peninsular War productions.

Goya also executed a number of bullfight paintings at different times throughout his artistic career, and the four (or five?) great lithographs popularly called *The Bulls of Bordeaux* (drawn in 1825 at that city during Goya's self-imposed exile from Spain; see page 77). At some point, probably early on, Goya made seven more bullfight aquatints of the same dimensions as the thirty-three in the 1816 edition; these were not published until 1876. They had been noticed etched on the backs of the *Tauromaquia* plates 1, 2, 6, 7, 11, 17 and 22, according to Tomás Harris, and may therefore be considered what the French call "planches refusées" (discarded subjects). These seven aquatints, generally known as numbers A through G, or 34A through 40G, of the *Tauromaquia,* are reproduced here from a set of the 1876 publication.

There are further *Tauromaquia* aquatint subjects usually not included in this series, rare proofs (some unique) in the Vienna Albertina and the Madrid Biblioteca Nacional; three of these are reproduced in this volume. Closely related to the *Tauromaquia* is the lovely "Lluvia de toros" (Rain of bulls), which properly belongs to the series of *Disparates* (published first under the title of *Los Proverbios* in 1864). Finally, there are a few odd lithographs and etchings on bullfight subjects that were never part of any series of which we know.

The *Tauromaquia* proper, of thirty-three aquatint plates (reproduced here from a set of the 1816 first edition),* begins with thirteen subjects which relate to the history of the sport long before Goya's lifetime; the rest are roughly contemporary subjects and often, one guesses, were either seen by Goya himself or were intimately described to him. These last, of course, are the most convincing and exciting. Splendid as it is to see "El Cid Campeador" (the famous *eleventh*-century Spanish hero) spearing a bull from the shoulder through the ribs (Plate 11), one is disappointed to find him attired in a *sixteenth*-century costume! Nor does the horseman of Plate 10 look like any known portrait of the Emperor Charles V. Rather, one can see that he is a glorified amplification of the rider in Pepe Illo's little 1804 *Tauromaquia,* Plate 7 (see Figure 1).† The "Moors" in Plates 3 through 8 are all unconvincing, but the landscape in Plate 2 wherein some "antiguos españoles" are hunting a bull on foot belongs to the finest, most luminous, scenes of this nature that Goya ever made.

Bound with complete sets of Goya's 1816 *Tauromaquia* series is a printed title page describing the subjects that Goya presumably thought he was illustrating. But, as has been seen, there were historical inaccuracies in these until Plate 14. Then the contemporary authentic scenes of Spain's national sport begin with a magnificent subject: a toreador who has just escaped the bull's charge by his quick footwork is watched by an impressionistically suggested audience in the grandstands that focuses one's attention on the two main protagonists.

The even greater agility of the bullfighter Juanito Apiñani is shown in Plate 20; he here performs a feat for which he was particularly noted. (Apiñani was active between 1750 and 1770, so the young Goya may easily have seen him in action.) Again Goya uses the audience in the background to direct attention to the perfectly timed vault. One more split second's reliance on the pole, and the torero would be brought down in the bull's path. This leap also demonstrates Goya's extraordinary eyesight in catching Apiñani's exact posture a good half-century before a fast-shuttered camera lens could prove that his vision was accurate.

Plate 21, "Death of the mayor of Torrejón," seems to this writer to be the finest single subject in the whole series, the climax of its dramatic confrontations. At the *corrida,* or bullfight, held on June 15, 1801 the fourth bull, from the famous herd of Palacios Rubios, broke through the barrier of the ring

*The engraved plate numbers have been omitted in this edition.

†It is also instructive to compare Plate 24 of Pepe Illo's little book (see Figure 2) with Goya's Plate 30 (the elements are reversed).

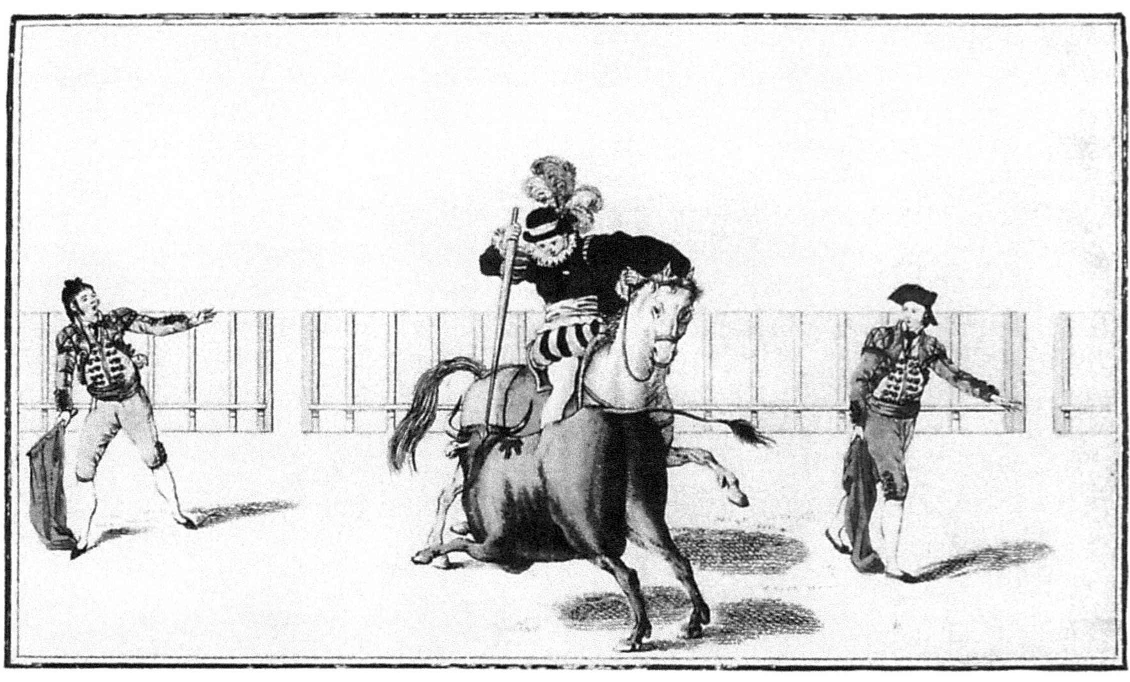

FIGURE 1

in Madrid and bolted up into the stands. The unfortunate mayor of Torrejón was in its path, and here, again, one finds an instantaneous record of what the artist must have seen with his own eyes. Goya's composition is unusually daring too. The right side of the scene is in pandemonium—the frenzied crowd contrasted with the momentarily static and triumphant bull. On the left, the stands are empty. Only the agonized face of one bullfighter peers over the heavy wooden fence dividing the ring from the grandstand, denying the apparent calm of the sunlit benches.

One could cite many other masterpieces in the published series, but it is harder to do this among the seven discarded subjects first published in 1876 at Paris, where Goya's copper plates had temporarily wandered before they were finally sold to the Círculo de Bellas Artes in Madrid (1921). Yet plate 38—marked as (extra plate) E by its publisher, Loizelet—has a dramatic scene very little inferior to Plate 32 of the first series, and the forty-first plate (Albertina), which is extremely rare—and was never published—is little inferior to Plate 18, for which it must have been a trial design.

The unpublished aquatint that Goya's bibliographer Loÿs Delteil lists next (not reproduced here), together with Plate 31 of the regular series, served Goya much later as a model for the most famous lithograph of his last productive period. "The divided ring" of *The Bulls of Bordeaux* series reproduces the important elements from each of these aquatints to supply the major elements in the two halves of that large print. This was a habit of Goya throughout his life. He did not mind repeating his own favorite ideas, and even whole compositions, any more than he found it improper to borrow the ideas of other artists, and to improve upon them.

There is plenty of vitality and violence in the *Tauromaquia* aquatints, but they are the only wholly reportorial Goya print series. They contain no fantastic imagination, nor any political or anticlerical meaning that can be observed.

Cambridge, Massachusetts
January 1969

PHILIP HOFER

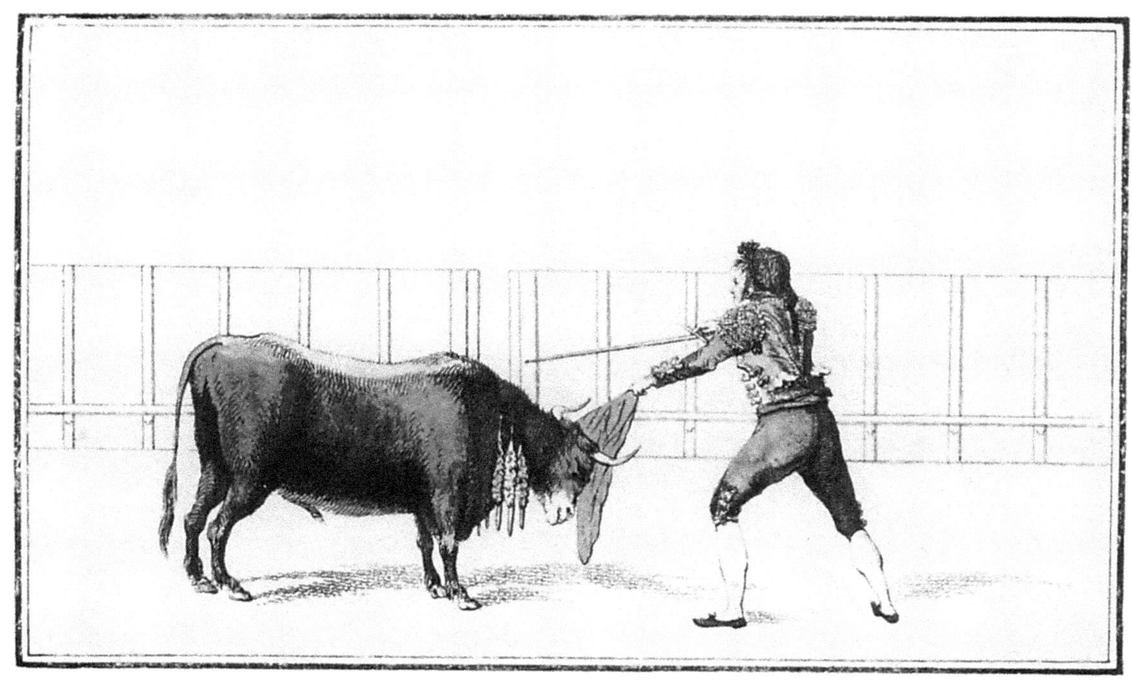

FIGURE 2

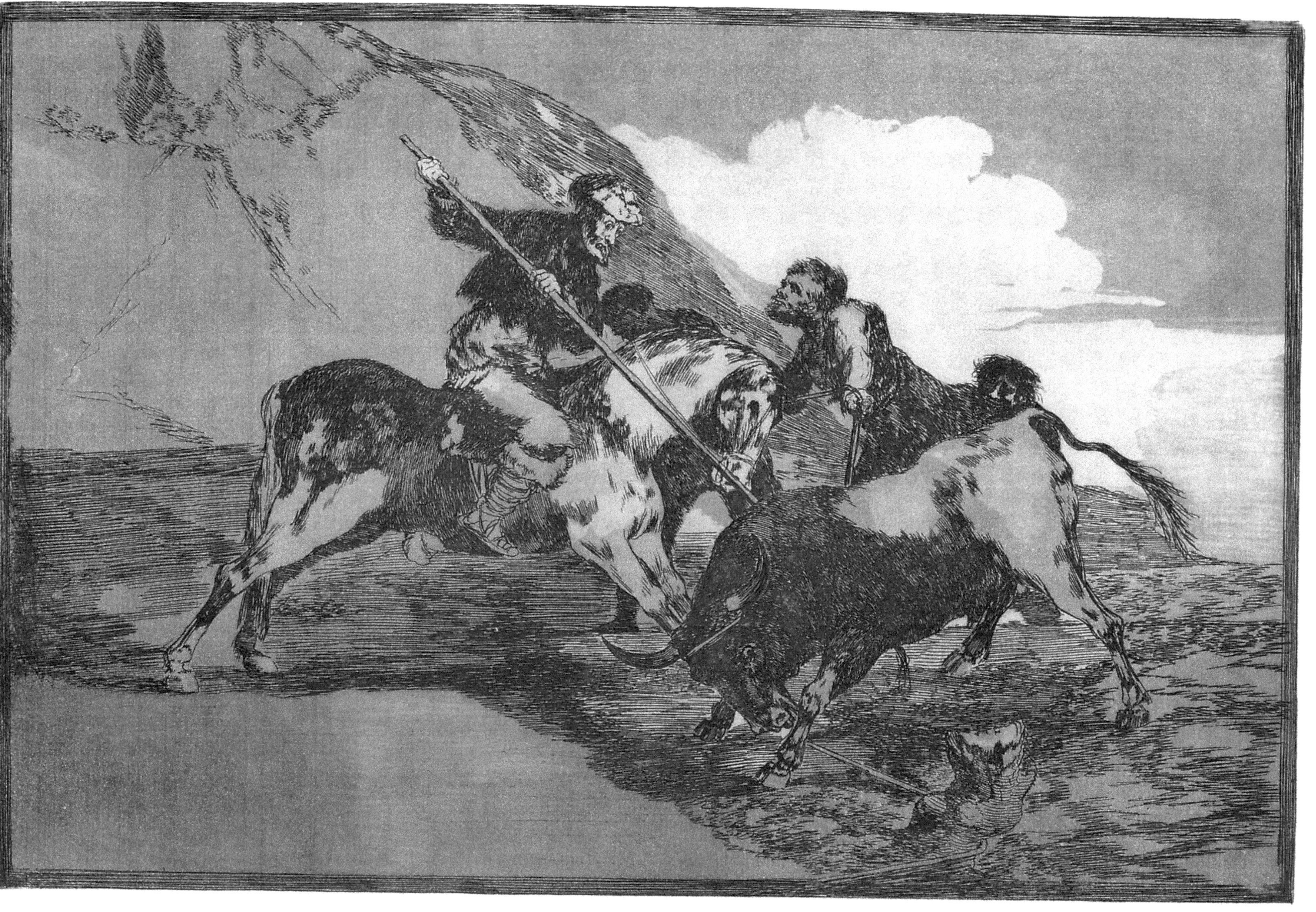

1 Modo con que los antiguos españoles cazaban los toros á caballo en el campo / *The way in which the ancient Spaniards hunted bulls on horseback in the open country*

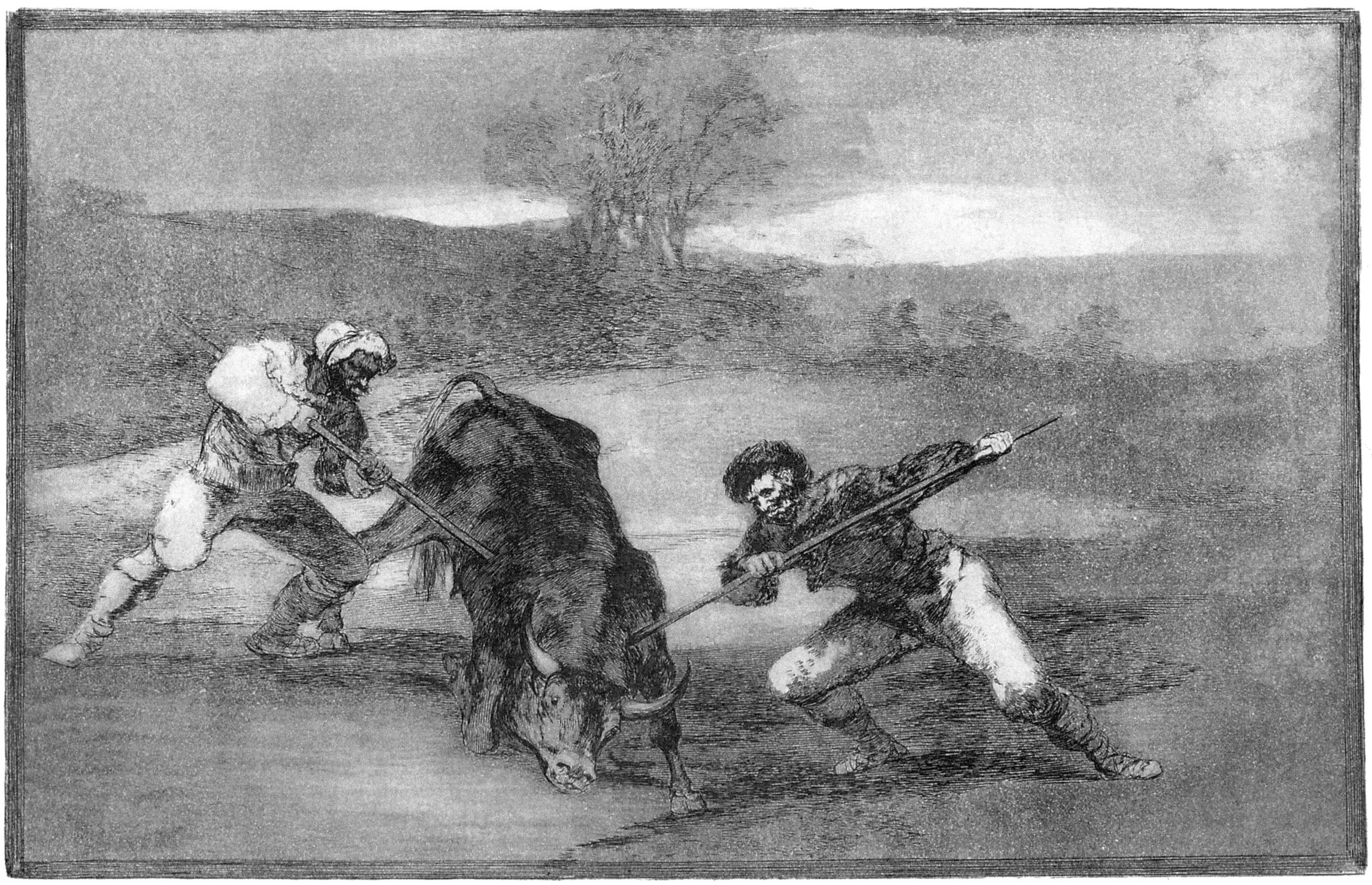

2 Otro modo de cazar á pie / *Another way of hunting on foot*

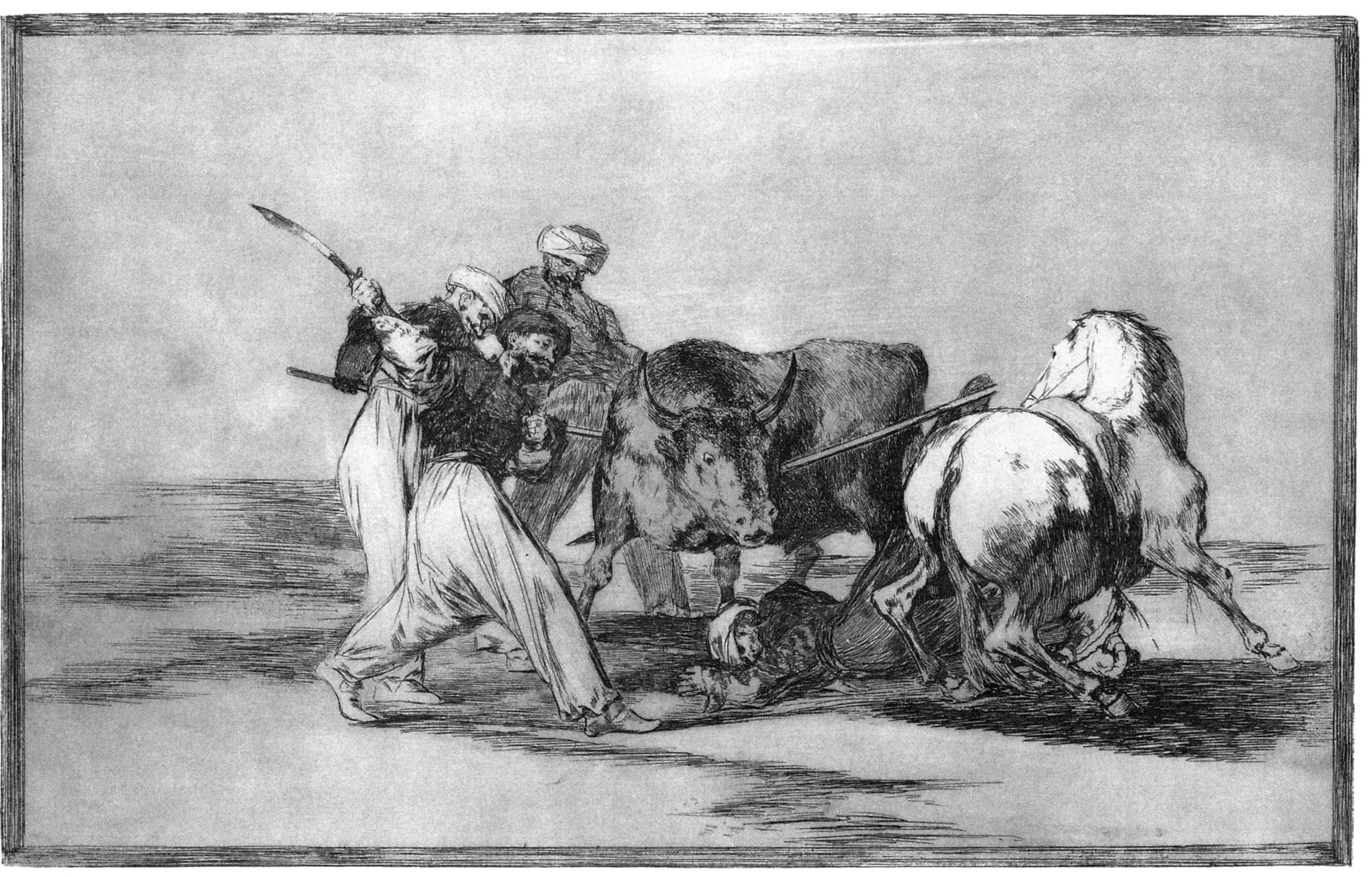

3 Los moros establecidos en España, prescindiendo de las supersticiones de su Alcorán, adoptaron esta caza y arte, y lancean un toro en el campo
The Moors settled in Spain, giving up the superstitions of the Koran, adopted this art of hunting, and spear a bull in the open

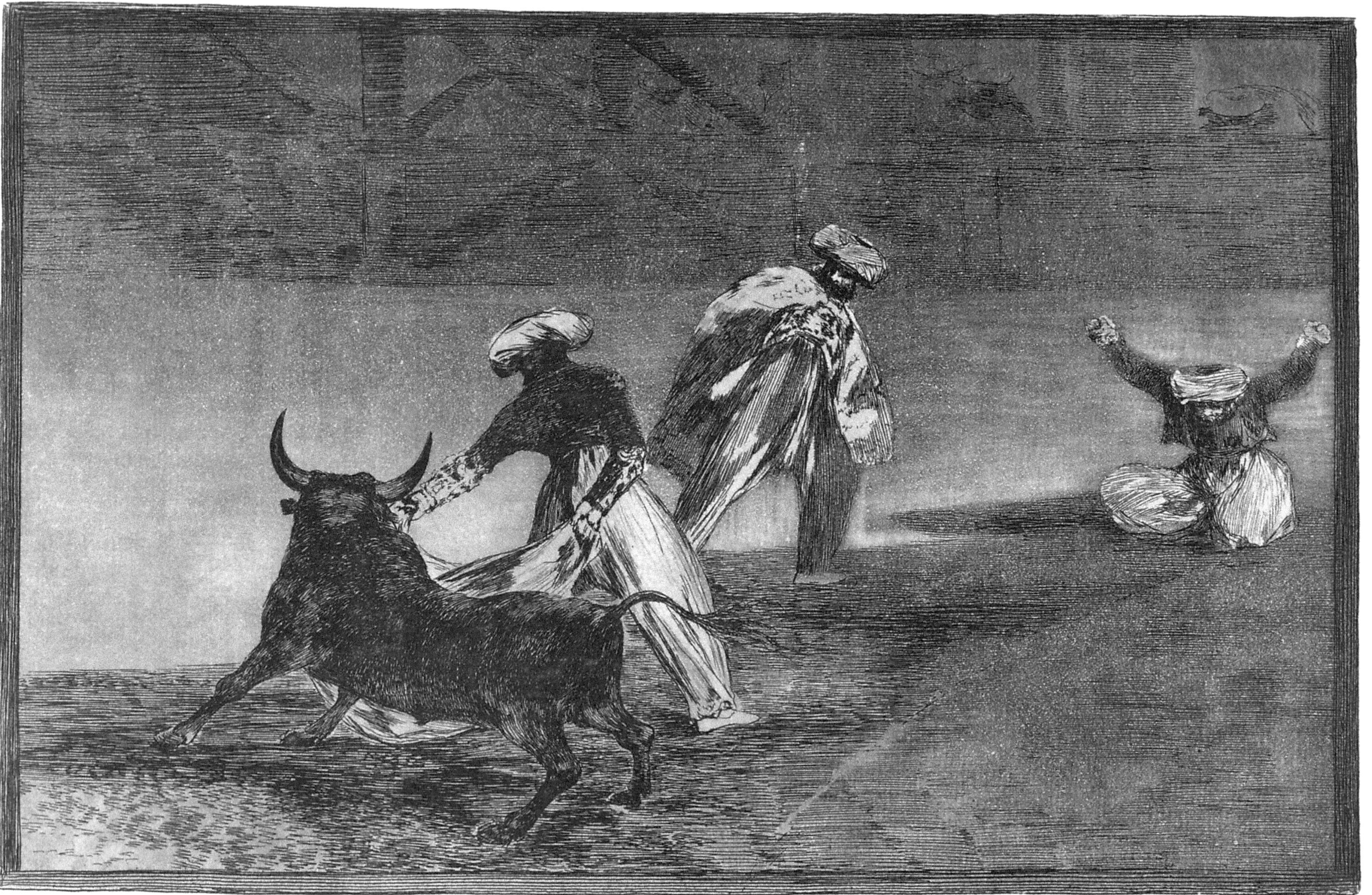

4 Capean otro encerrado / *They play another with the cape in an enclosure*

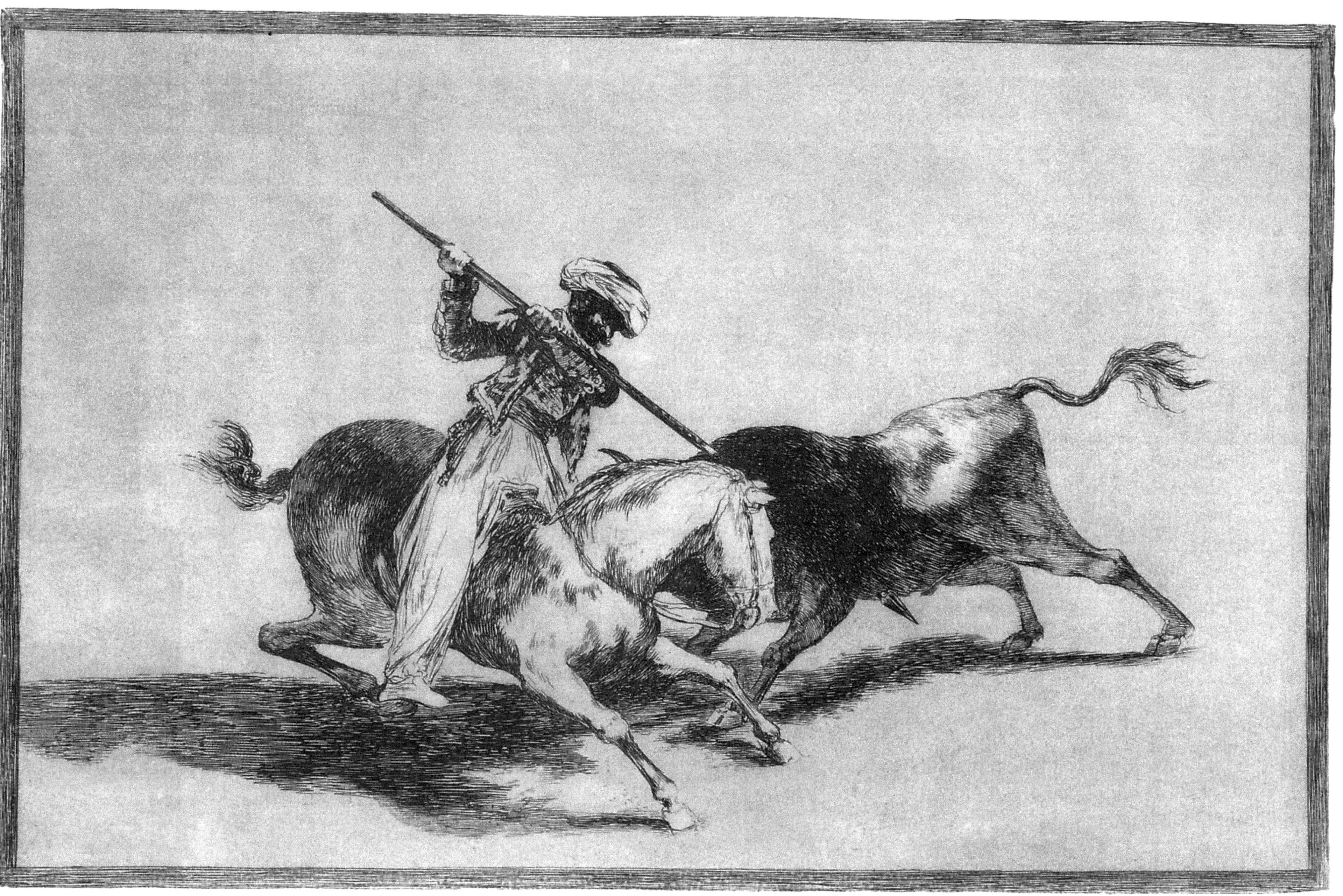

5 El animoso moro Gazul es el primero que lanceó toros en regla / *The spirited Moor Gazul is the first to spear bulls according to rules*

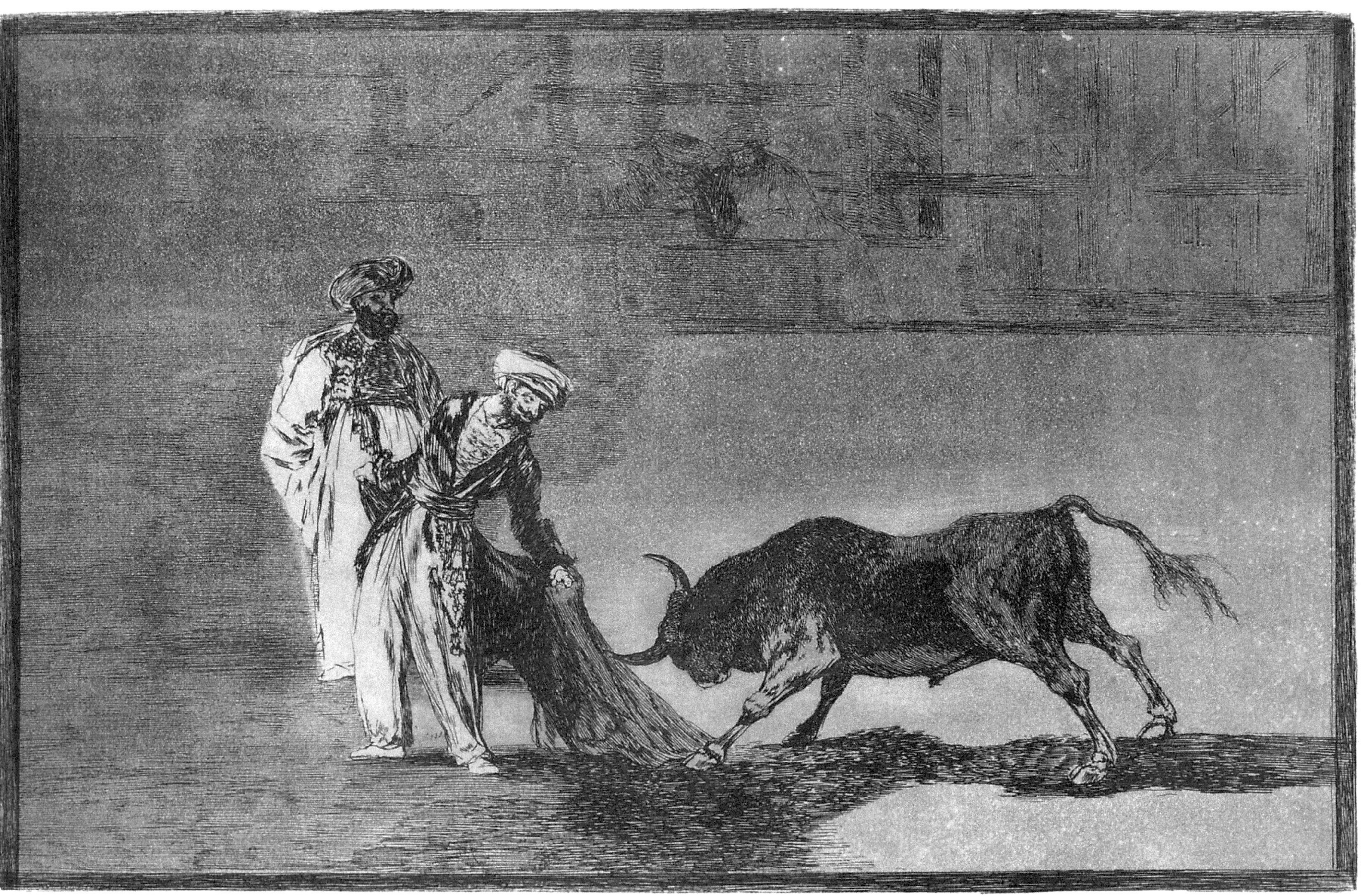

6 Los moros hacen otro capeo en plaza con su albornoz / *The Moors make a different play in the ring calling the bull with their burnous*

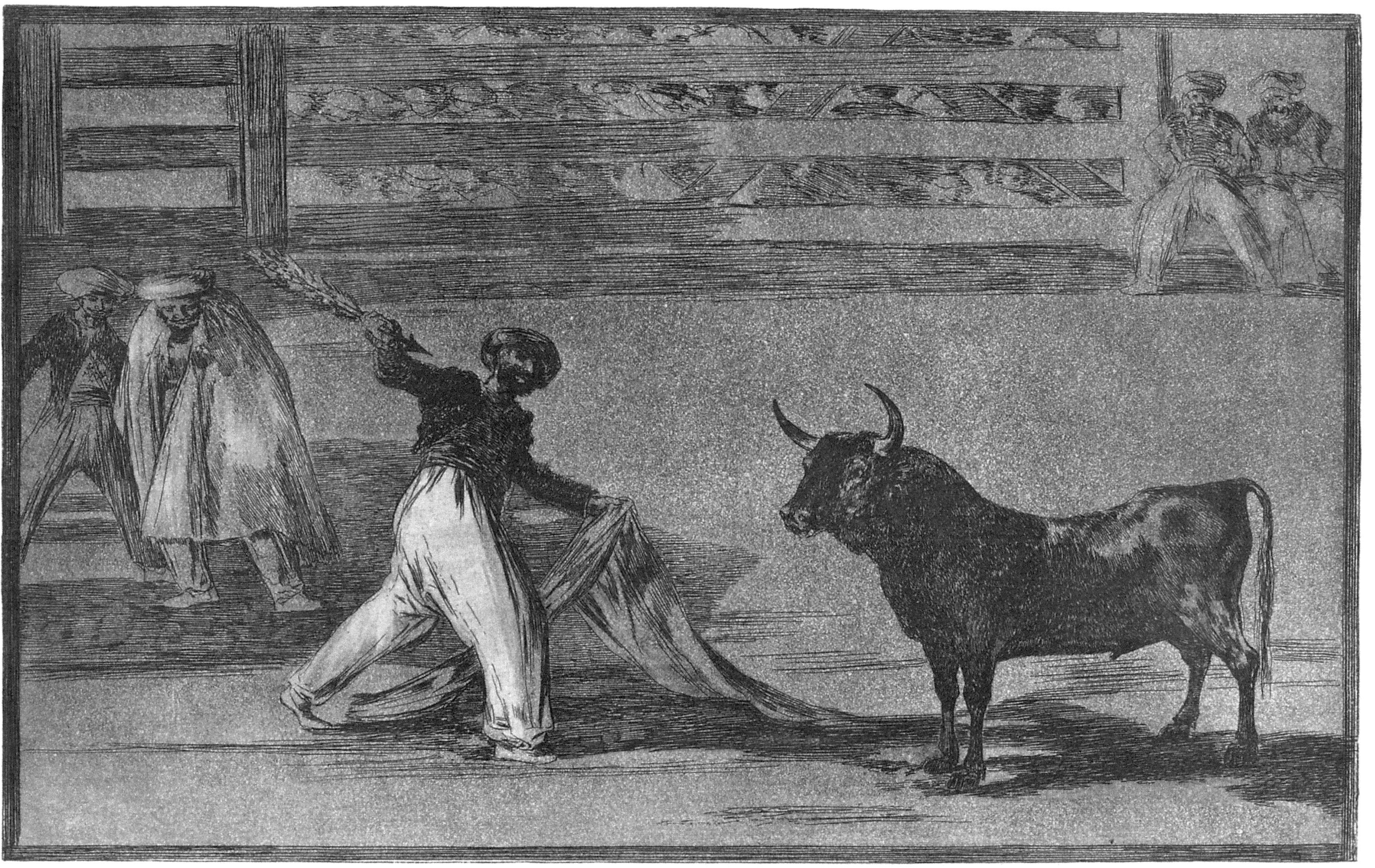

7 ORIGEN DE LOS ARPONES Ó BANDERILLAS / *Origin of the harpoons or banderillas*

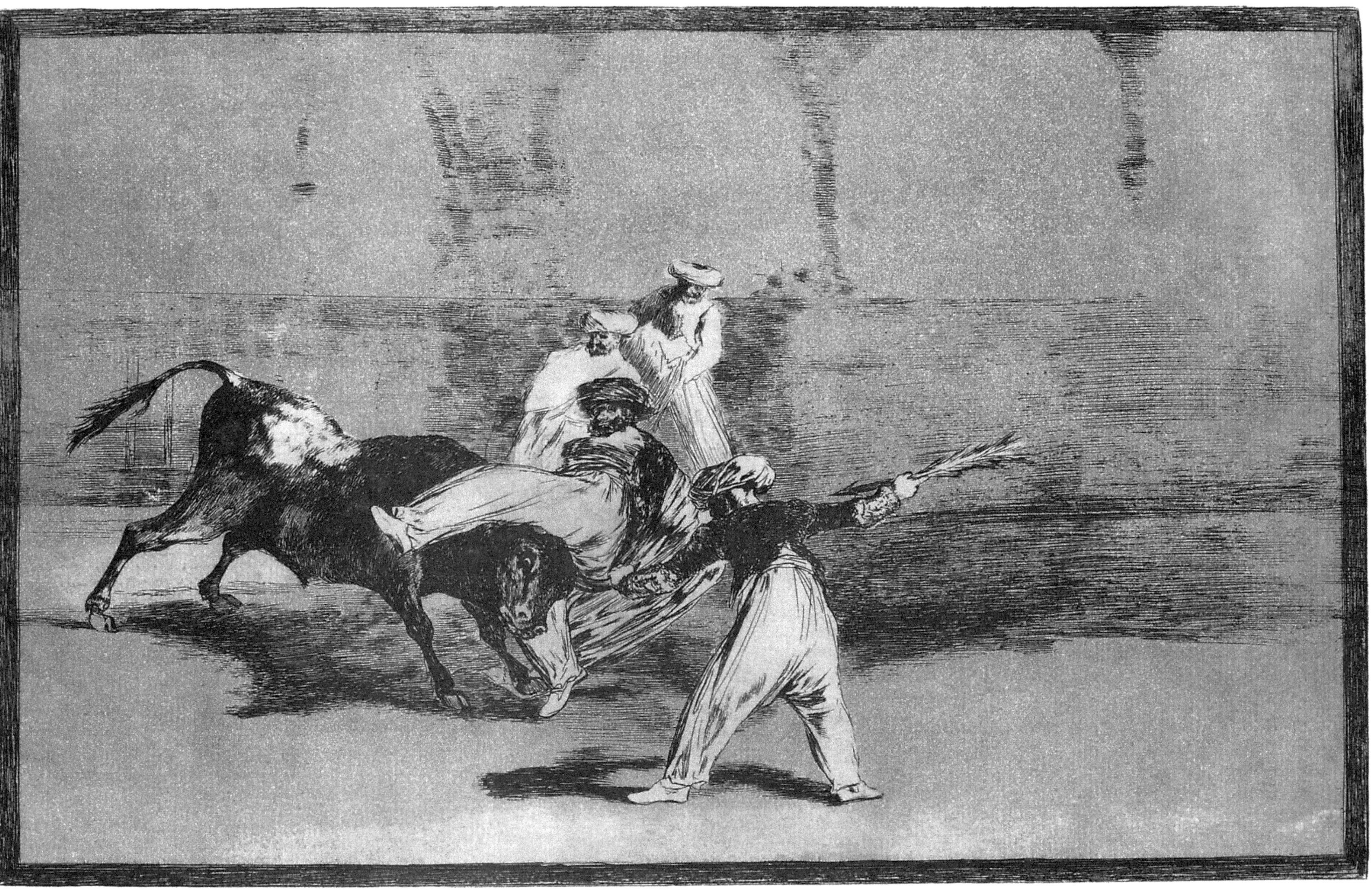

8 Cogida de un moro estando en la plaza / *A Moor caught by the bull in the ring*

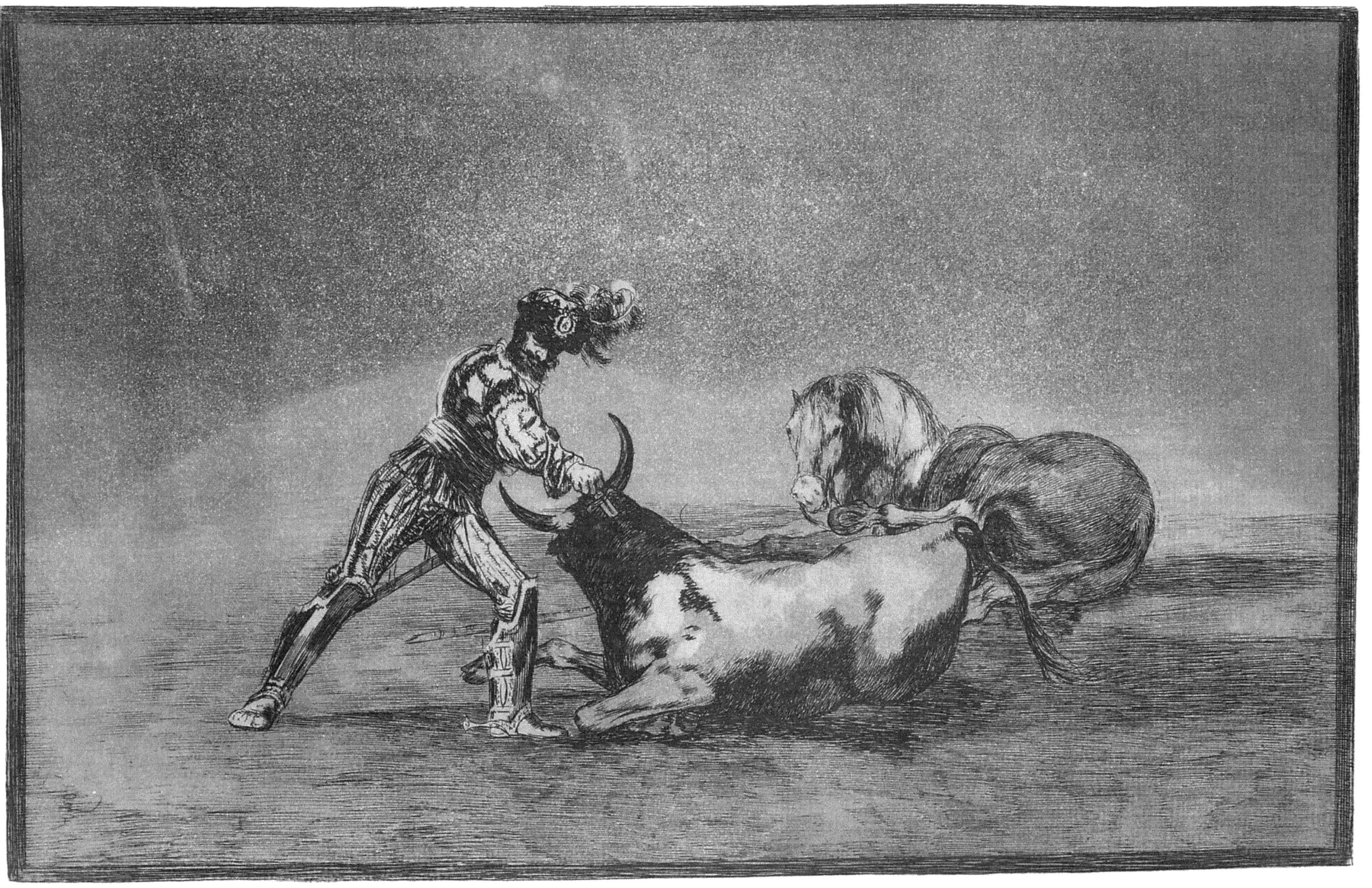

9 Un caballero español mata un toro despues de haber perdido el caballo / *A Spanish knight kills the bull after having lost his horse*

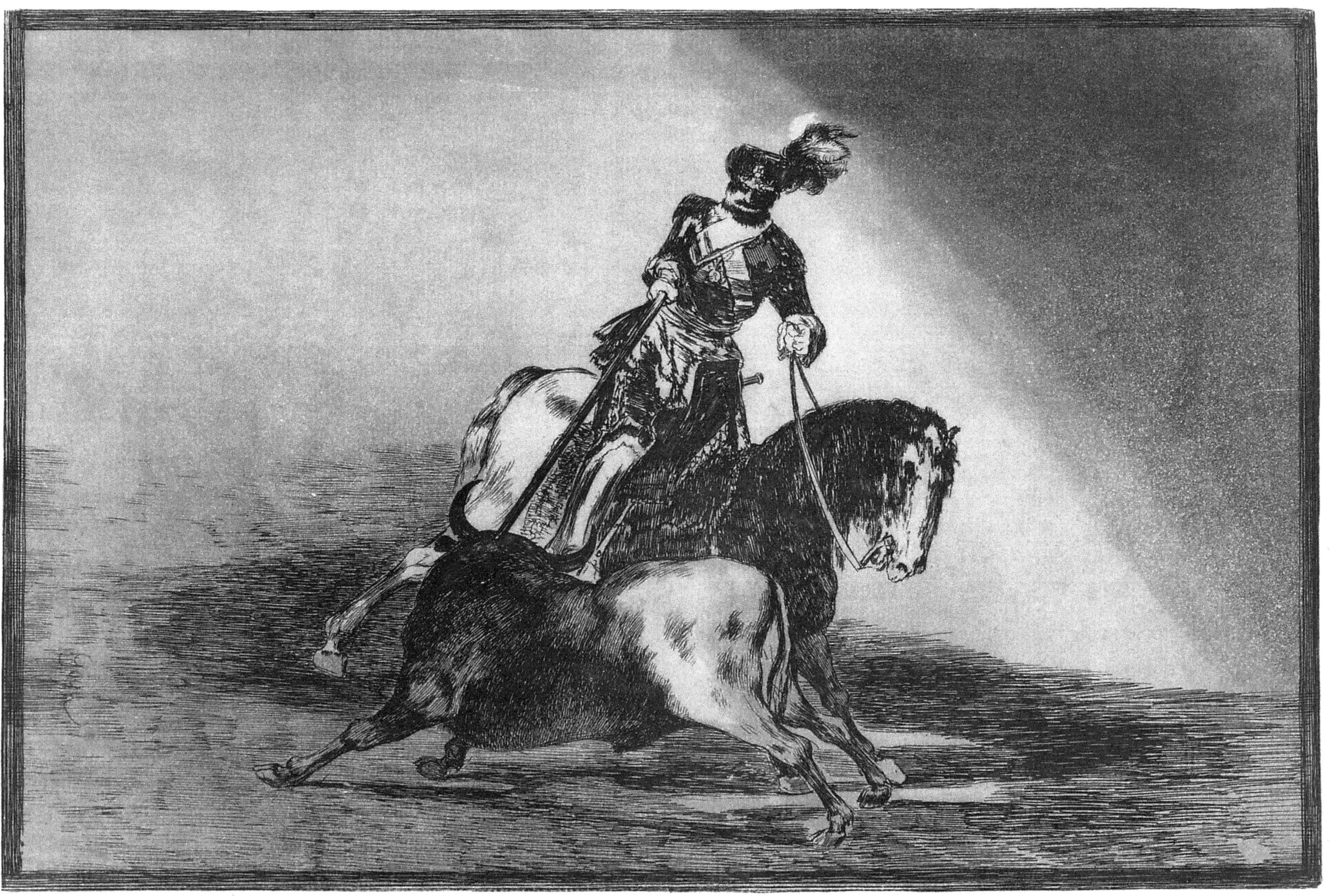

10 Carlos V. lanceando un toro en la plaza de Valladolid / *Charles V spearing a bull in the ring at Valladolid*

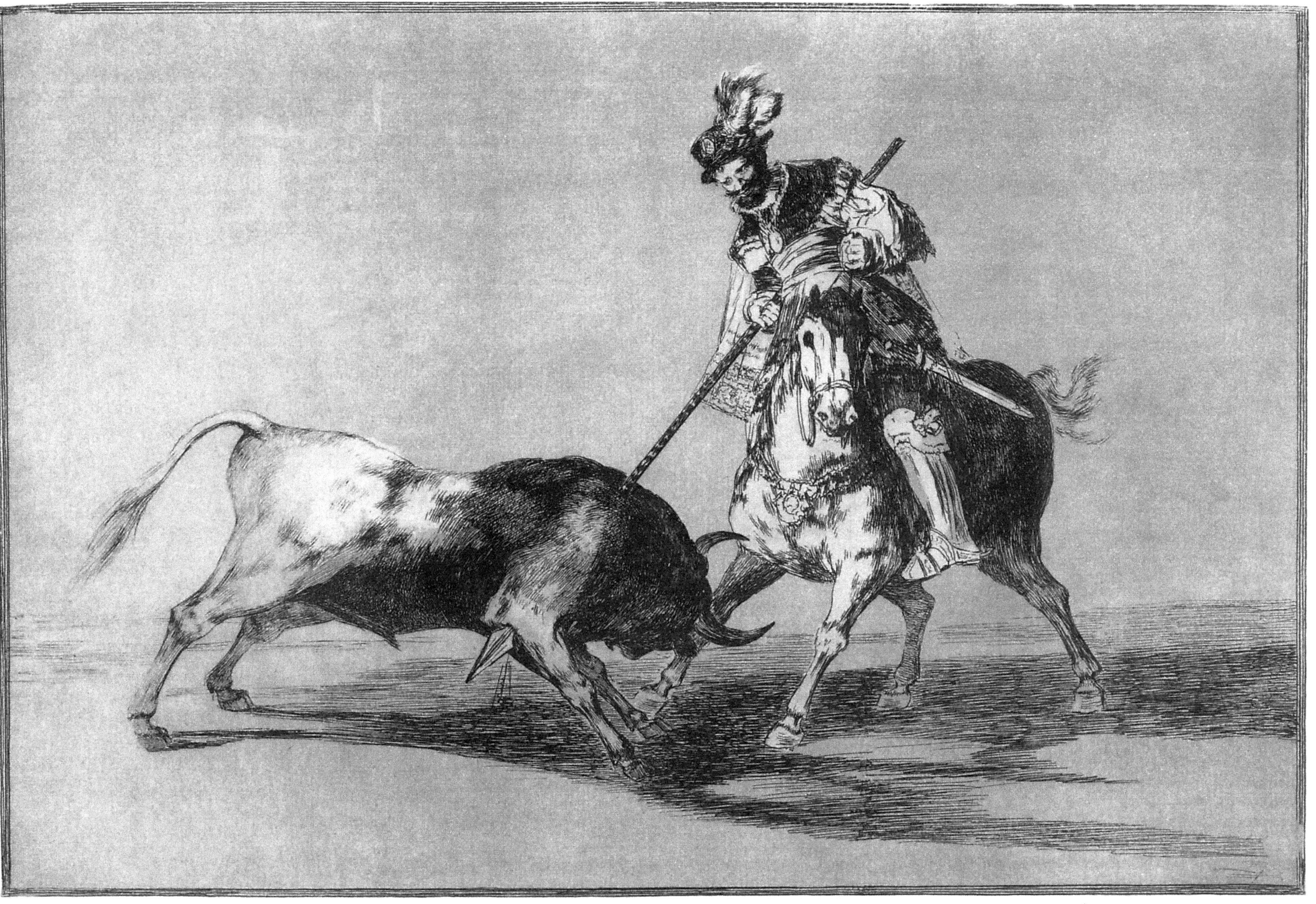

11 El Cid Campeador lanceando otro toro / *The Cid Campeador spearing another bull*

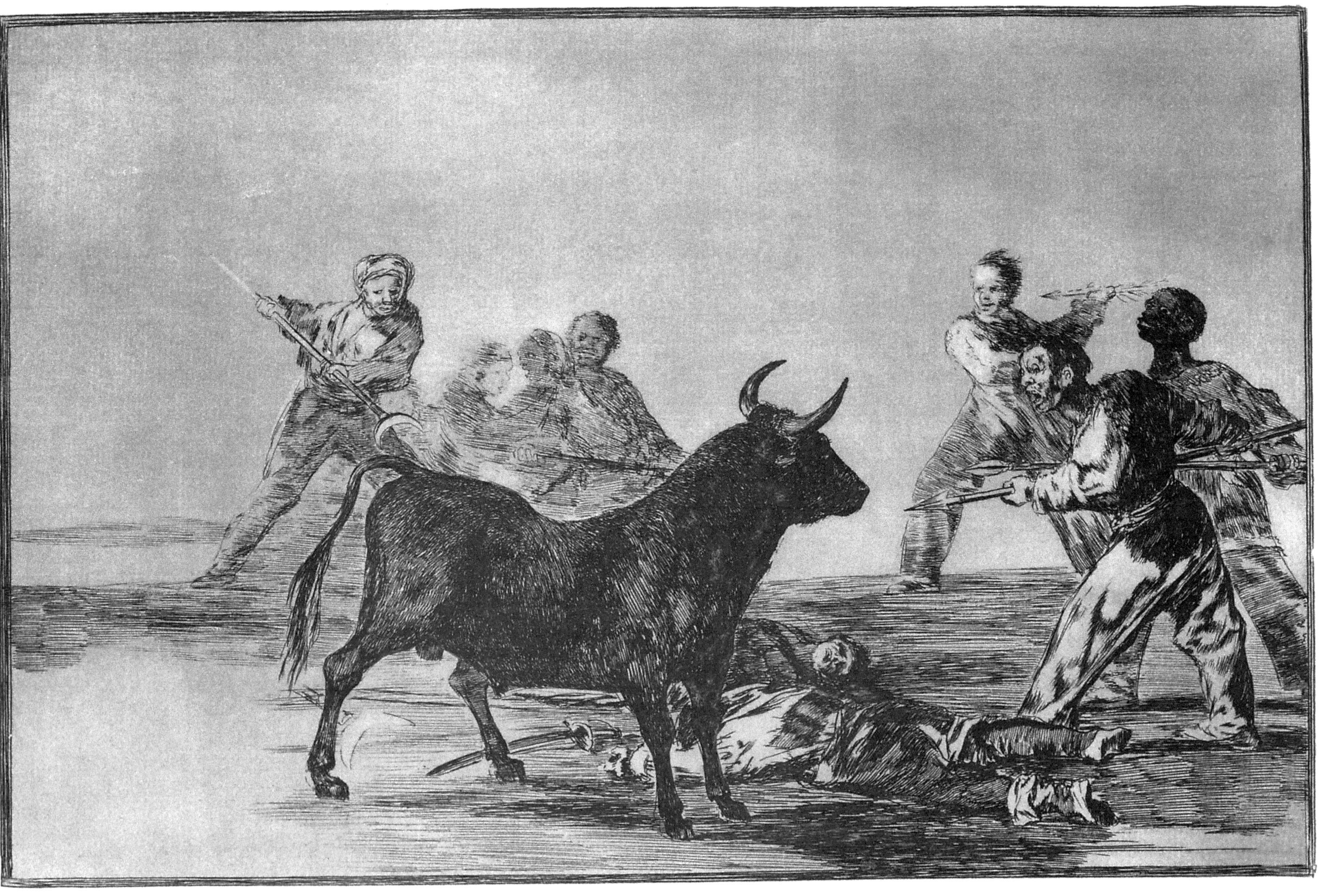

12 Desjarrete de la canalla con lanzas, medias-lunas, banderillas y otras armas / *The rabble hamstring the bull with lances, sickles, banderillas and other arms*

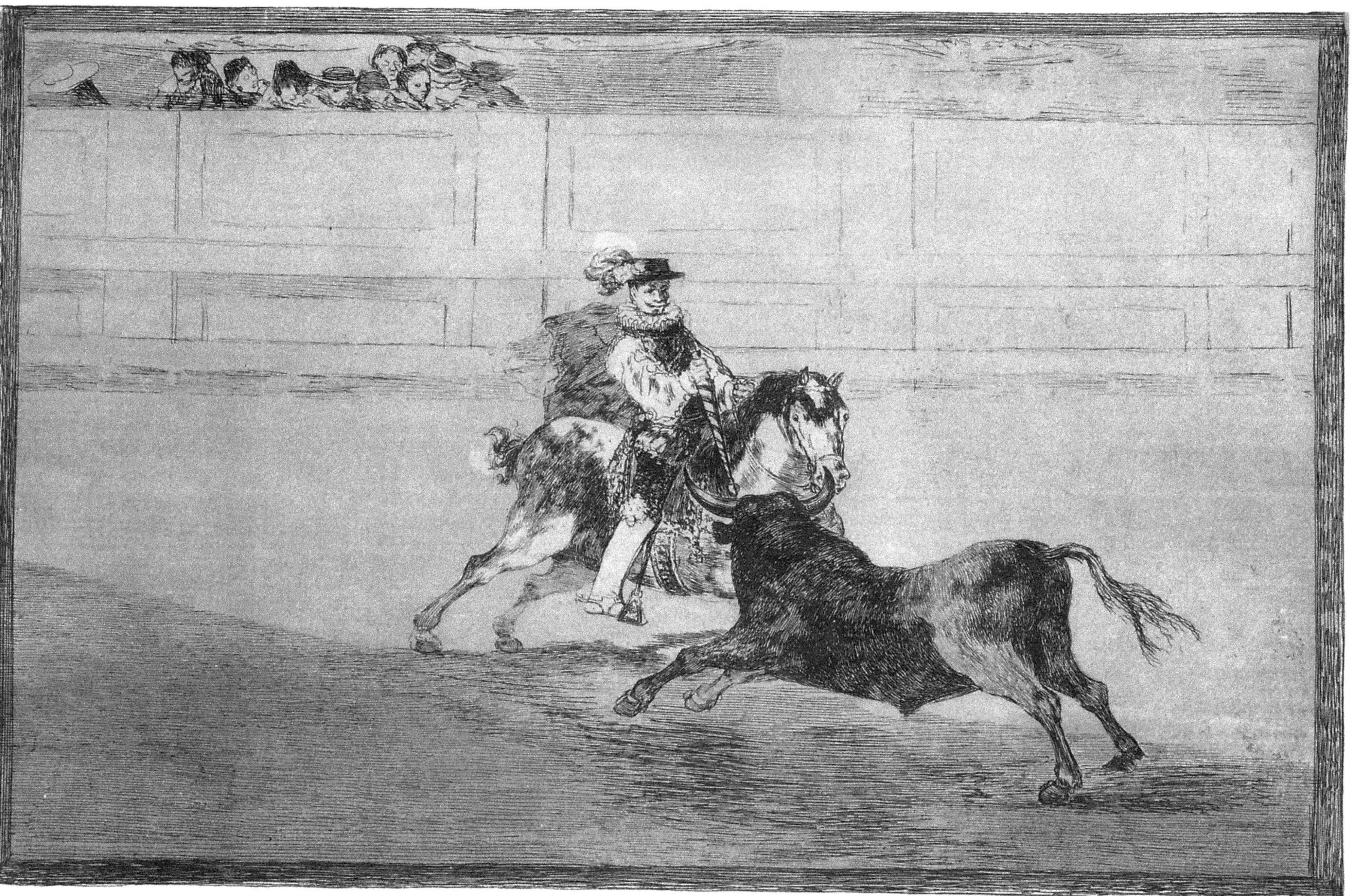

13 Un caballero español en plaza quebrando rejoncillos sin auxilio de los chulos / *A Spanish mounted knight in the ring breaking short spears without the help of assistants*

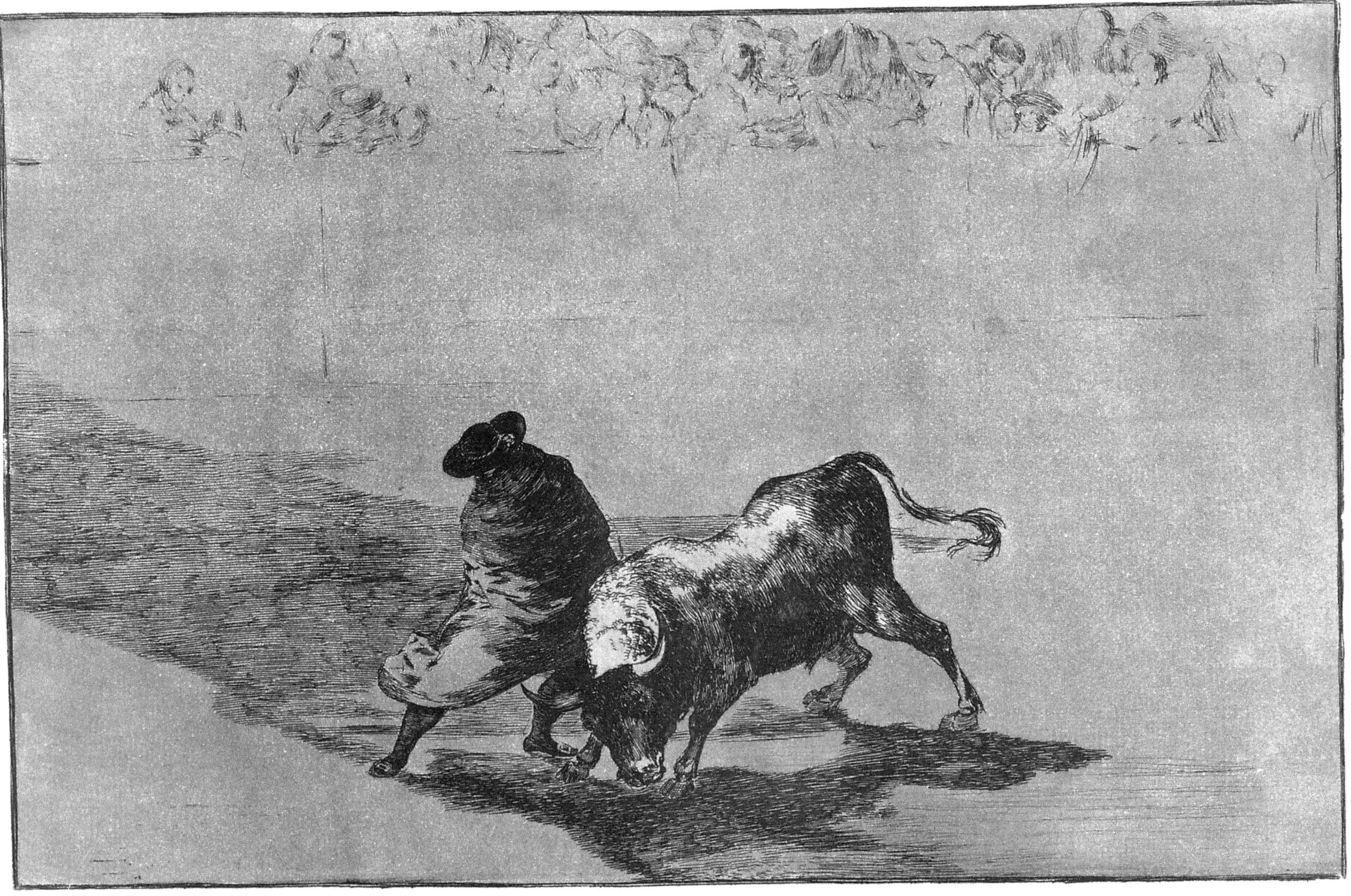

14 El diestrísimo estudiante de Falces, embozado burla al toro con sus quiebros / *The very skillful student of Falces, wrapped in his cape, tricks the bull with the play of his body*

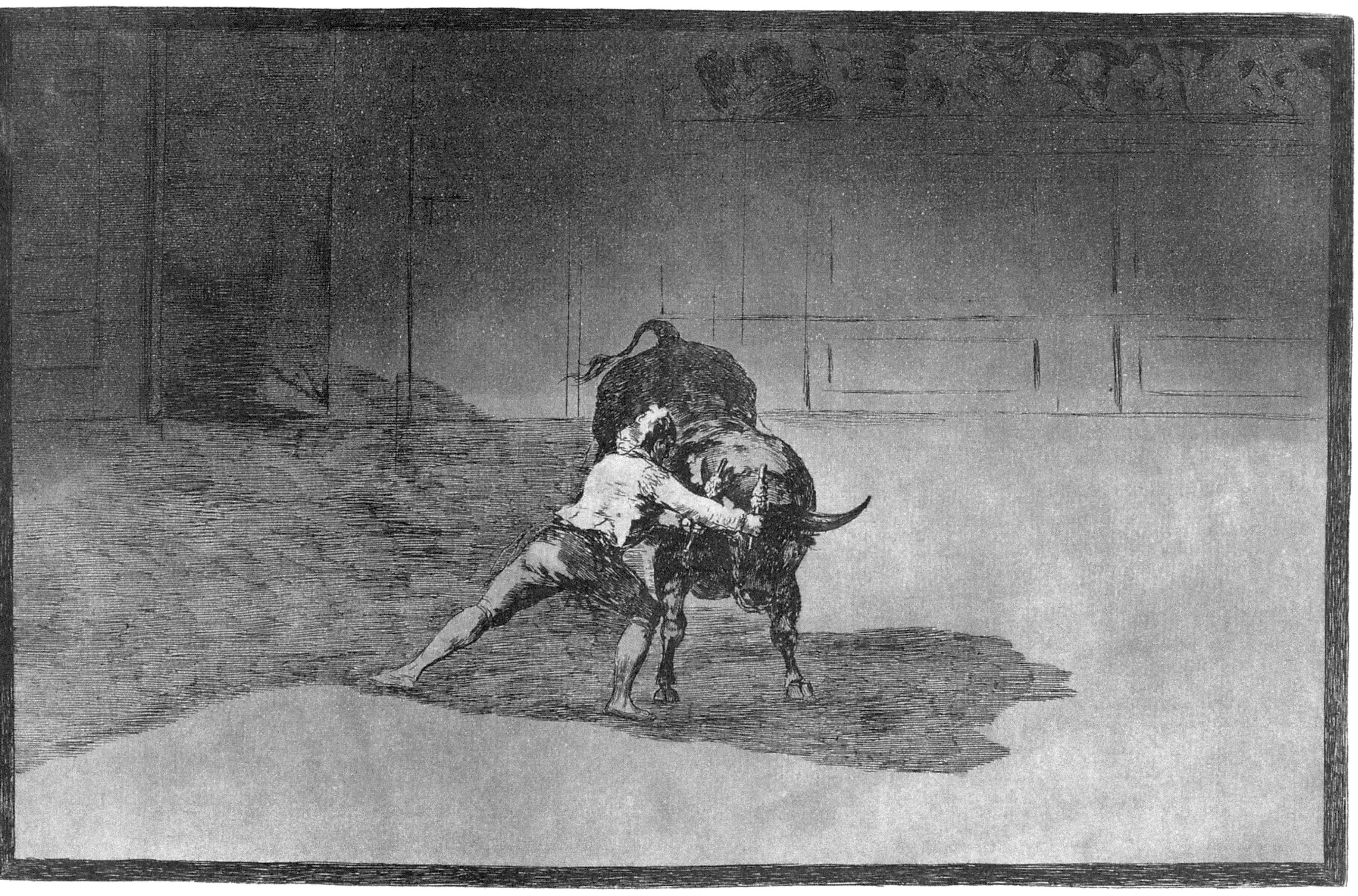

15 El famoso Martincho poniendo banderillas al quiebro / *The famous Martincho places the banderillas, playing the bull with the movement of his body*

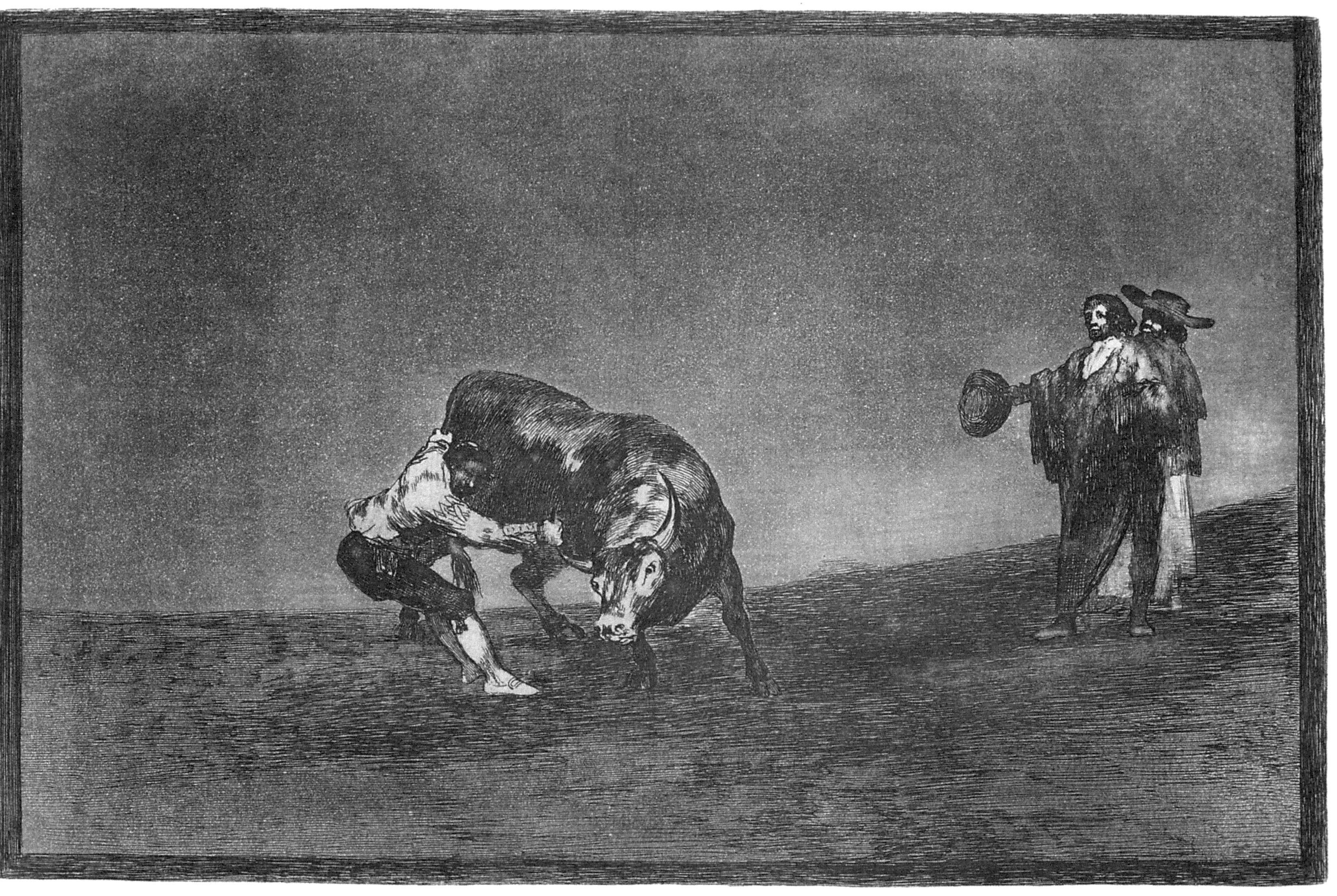

16 El mismo vuelca un toro en la plaza de Madrid / *The same man throws a bull in the ring at Madrid*

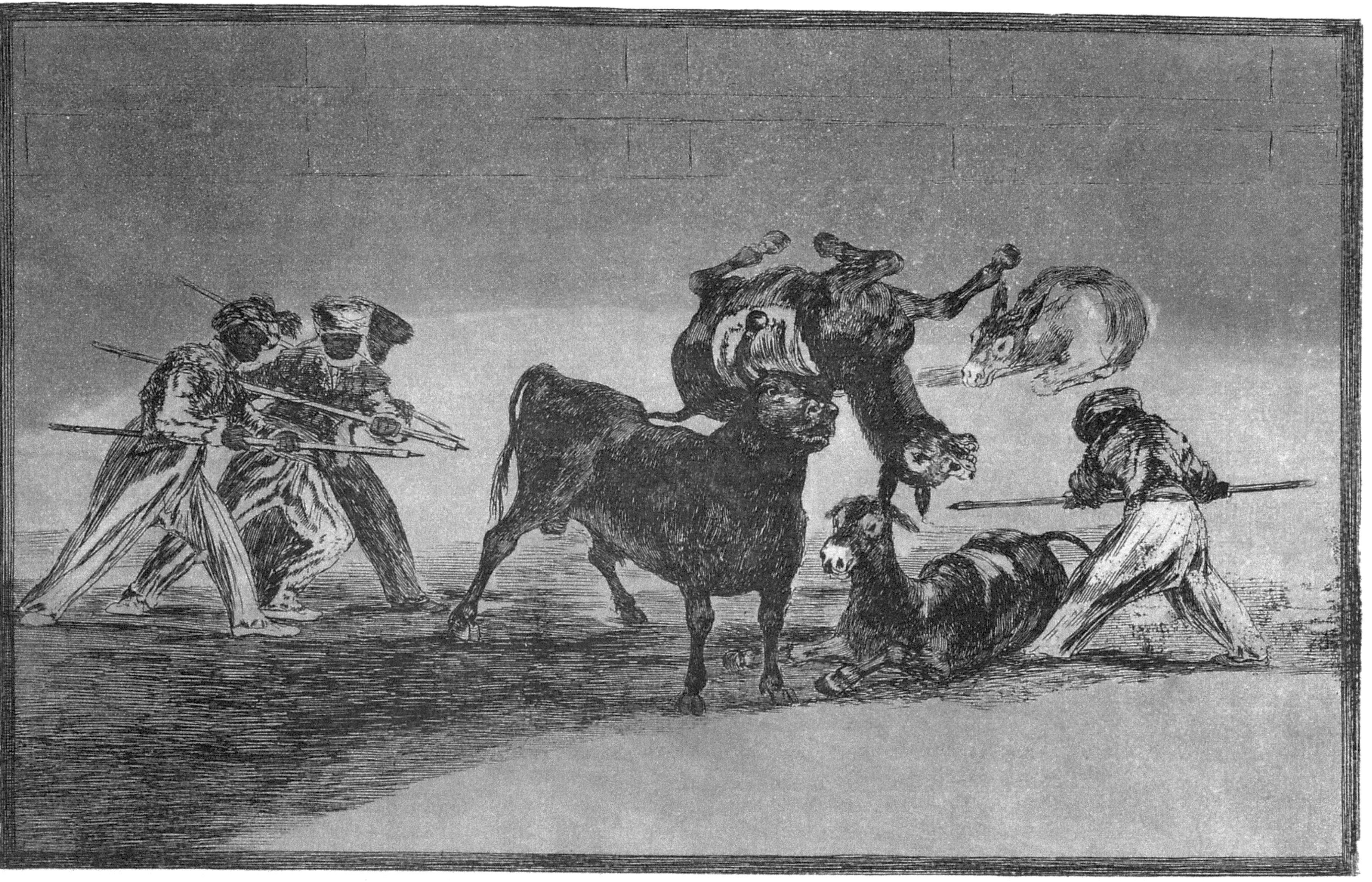

17 PALENQUE DE LOS MOROS HECHO CON BURROS PARA DEFENDERSE DEL TORO EMBOLADO
The Moors use donkeys as a barrier to defend themselves against the bull whose horns have been tipped with balls

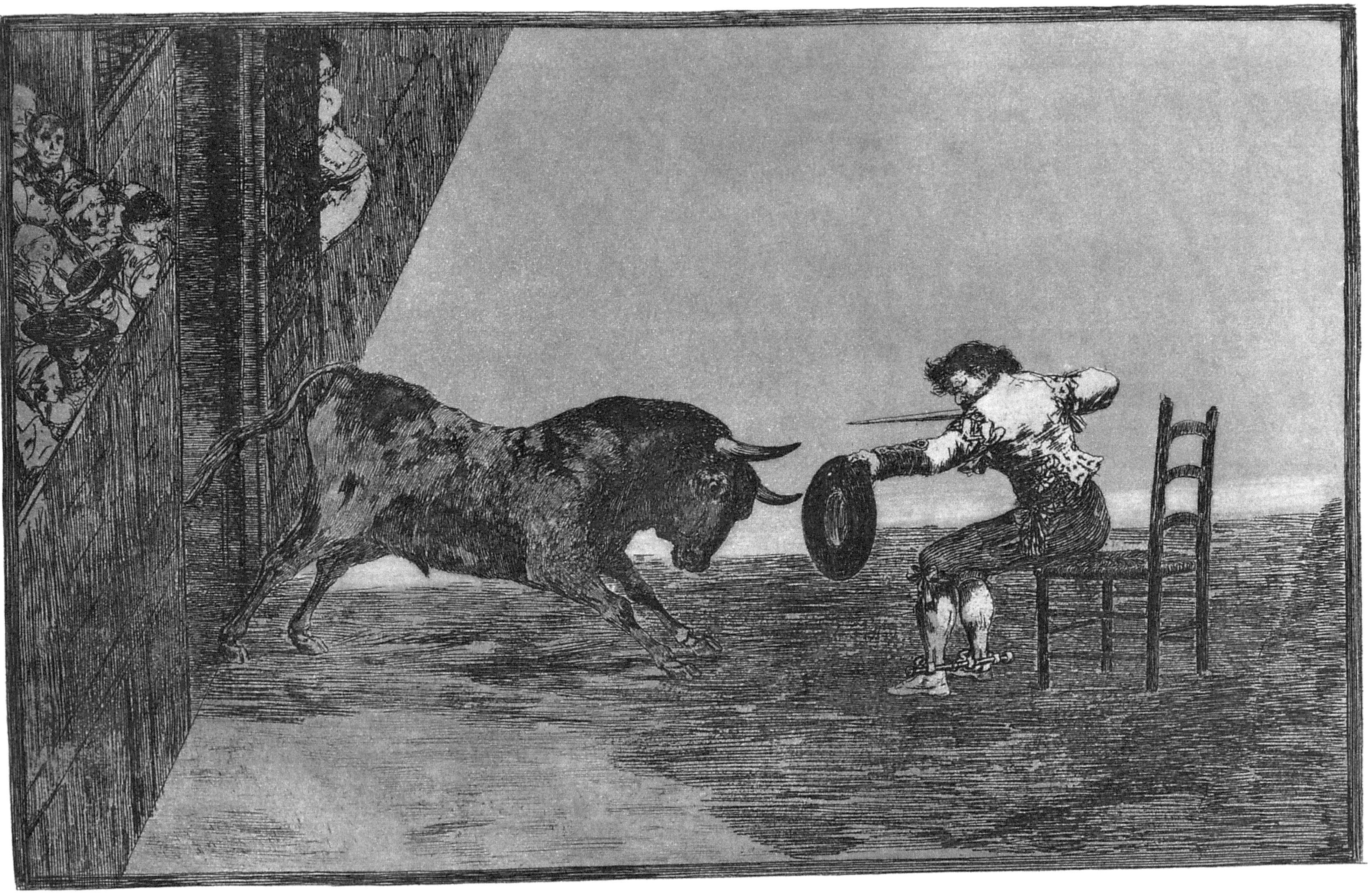

18 Temeridad de Martincho en la plaza de Zaragoza / *The daring of Martincho in the ring at Saragossa*

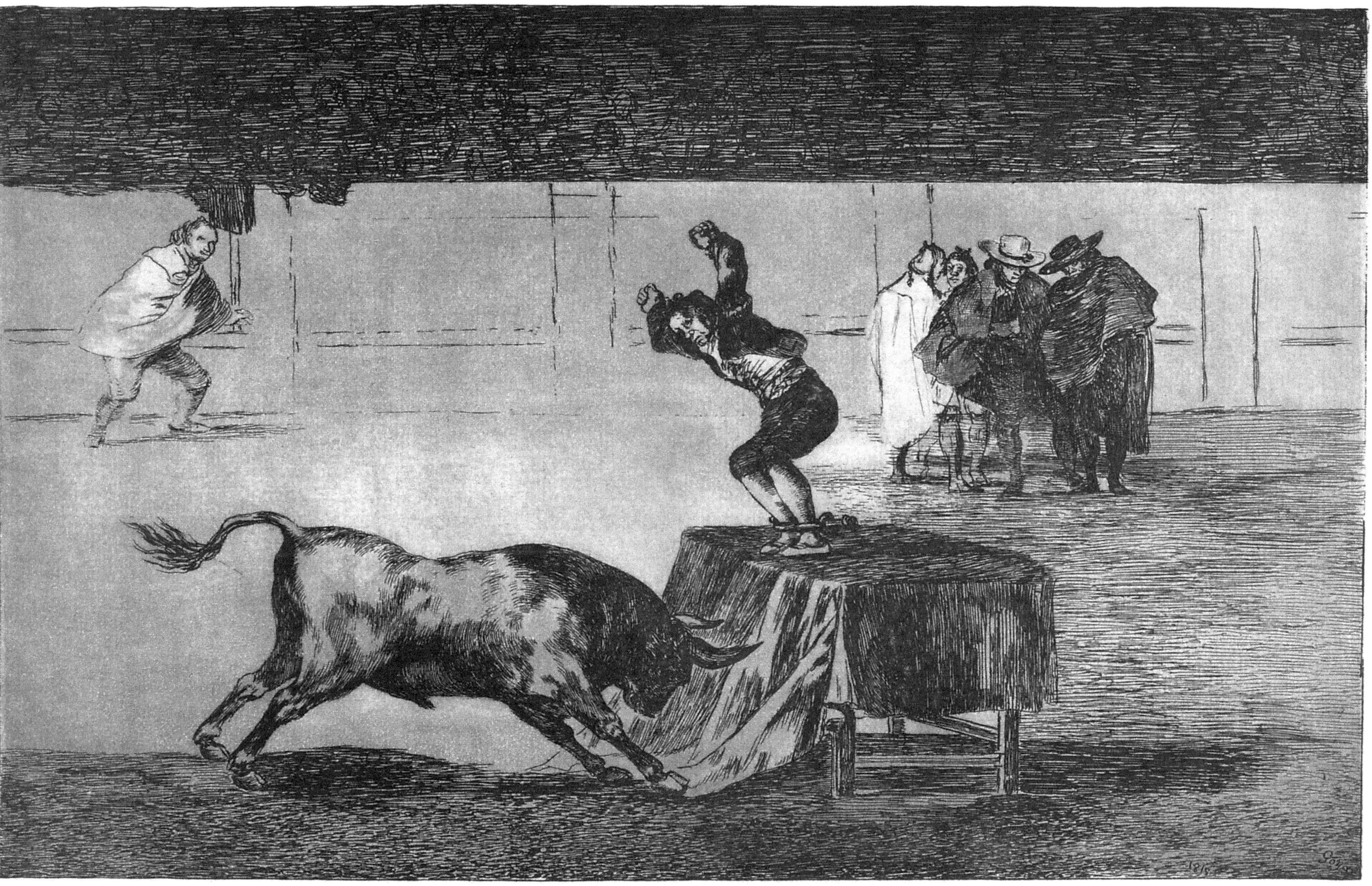

19 Otra locura suya en la misma plaza / *Another madness of his in the same ring*

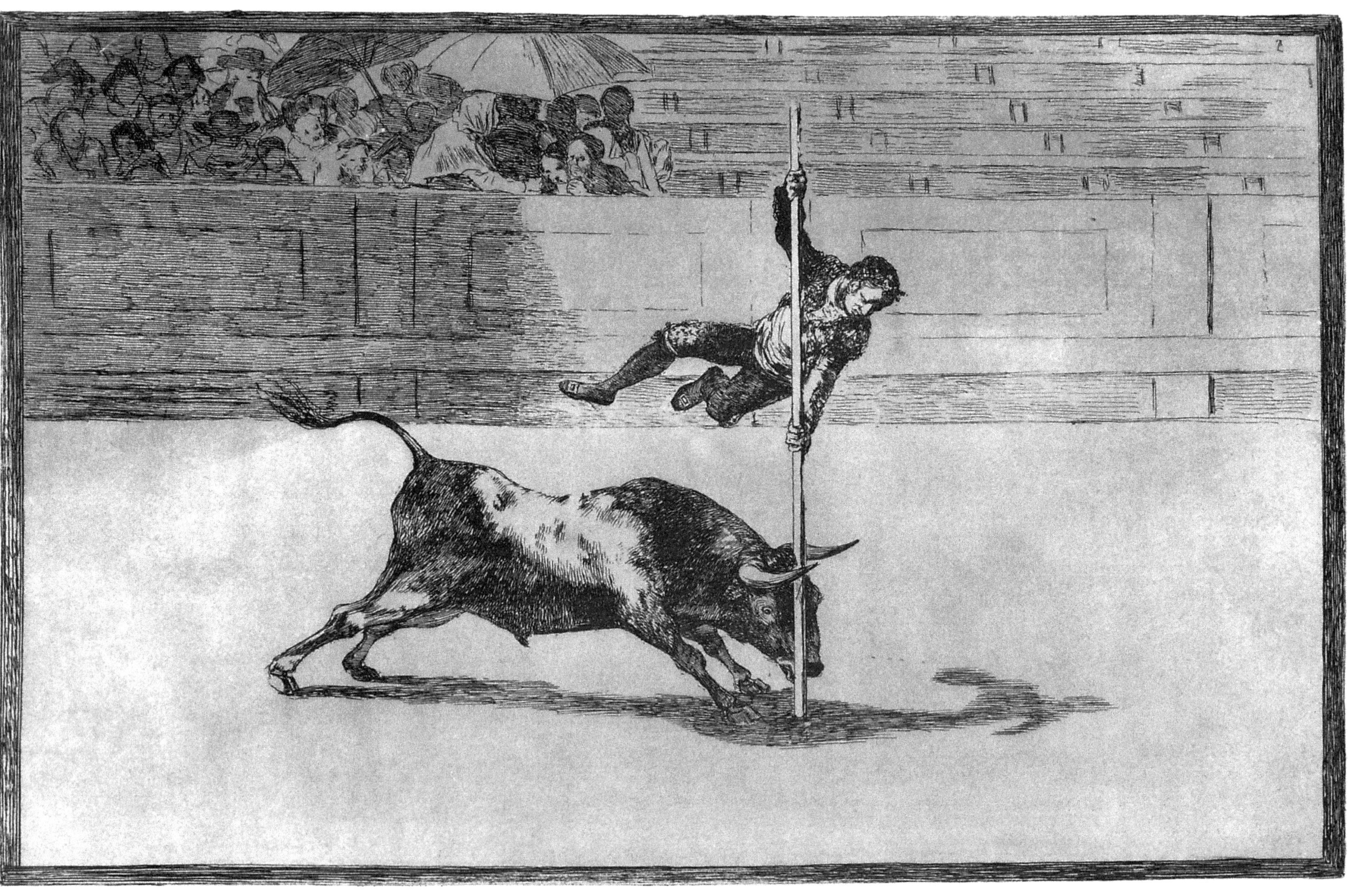

20 Ligereza y atrevimiento de Juanito Apiñani en la de Madrid / *The agility and audacity of Juanito Apiñani in [the ring] at Madrid*

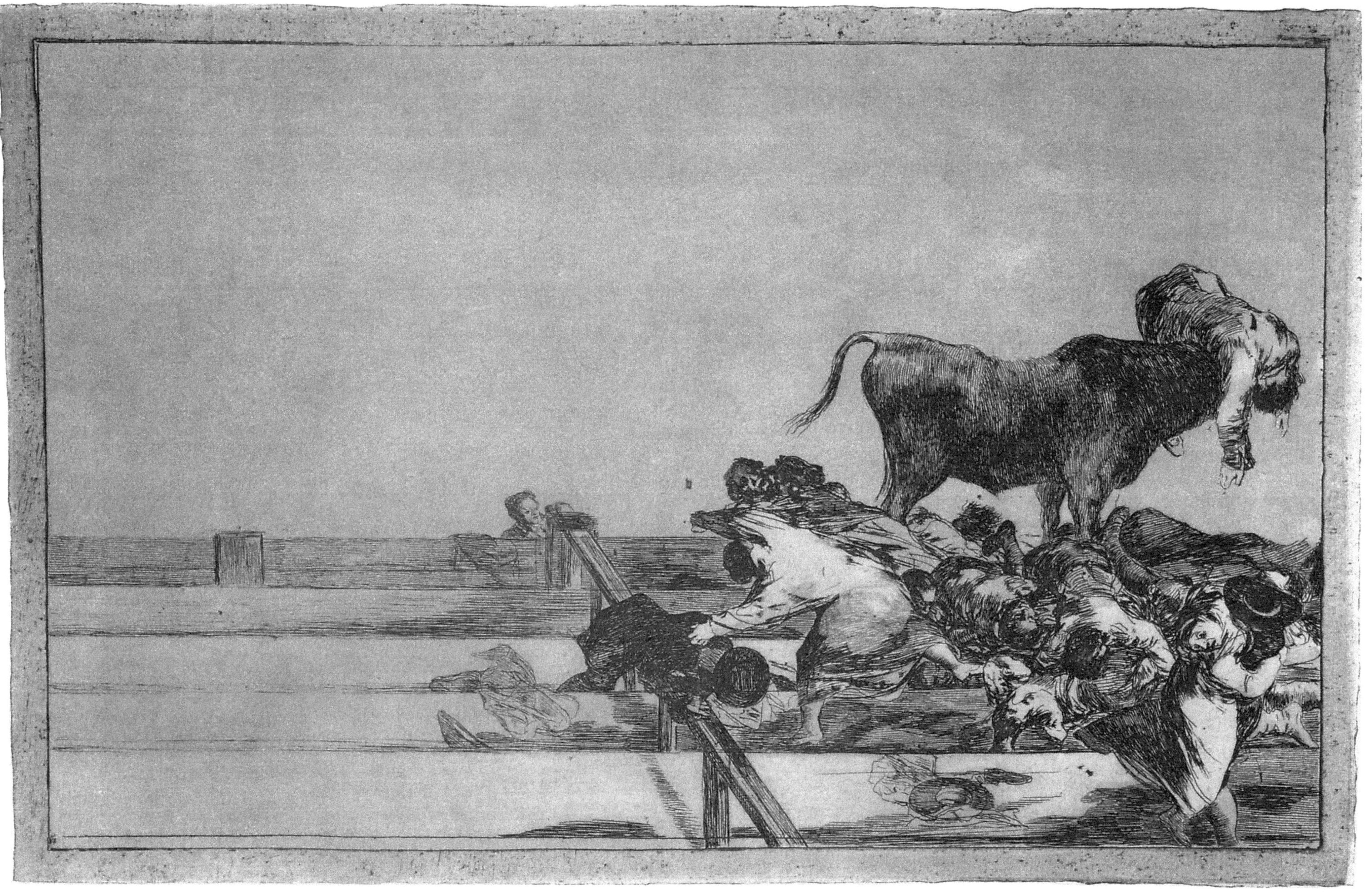

21 Desgracias acaecidas en el tendido de la plaza de Madrid, y muerte del alcalde de Torrejon / *Dreadful events in the front rows of the ring at Madrid and death of the mayor of Torrejon*

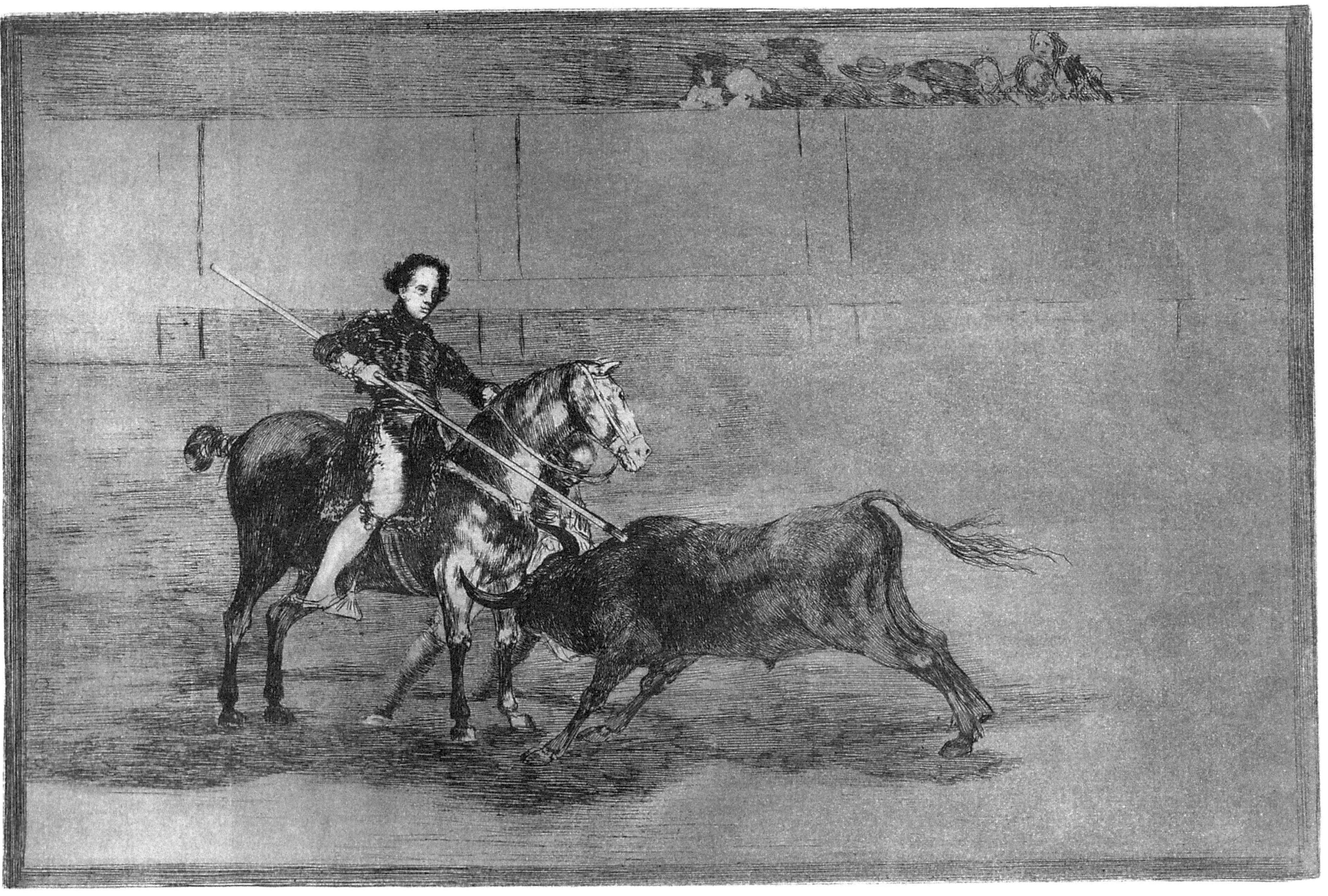

22 Valor varonil de la célebre Pajuelera en la de Zaragoza / *Manly courage of the celebrated Pajuelera in [the ring] at Saragossa*

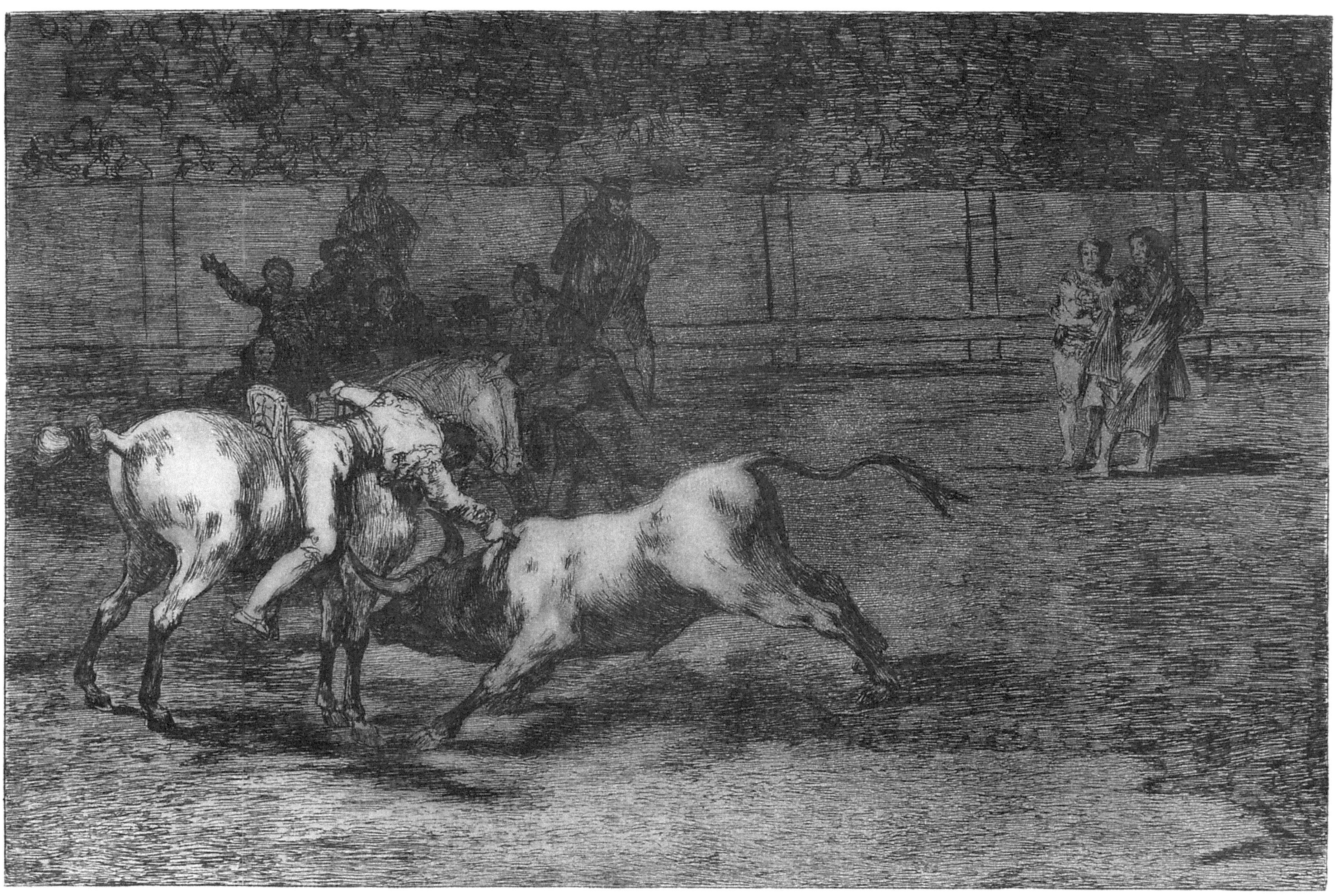

23 Mariano Ceballos, alias el Indio, mata el toro desde su caballo / *Mariano Ceballos, alias the Indian, kills the bull from his horse*

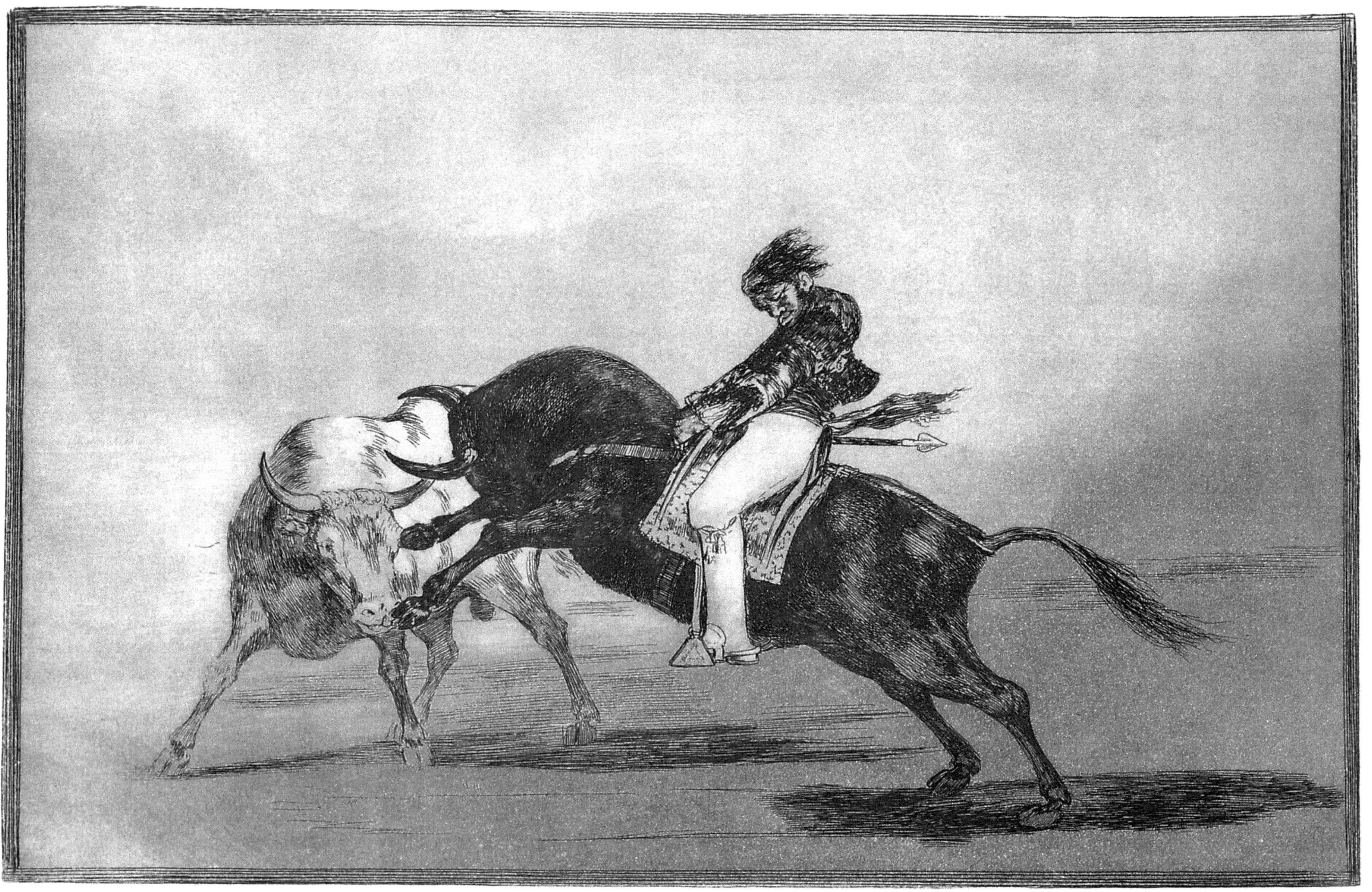

24 El mismo Ceballos montado sobre otro toro quiebra rejones en la plaza de Madrid / *The same Ceballos mounted on another bull breaks short spears in the ring at Madrid*

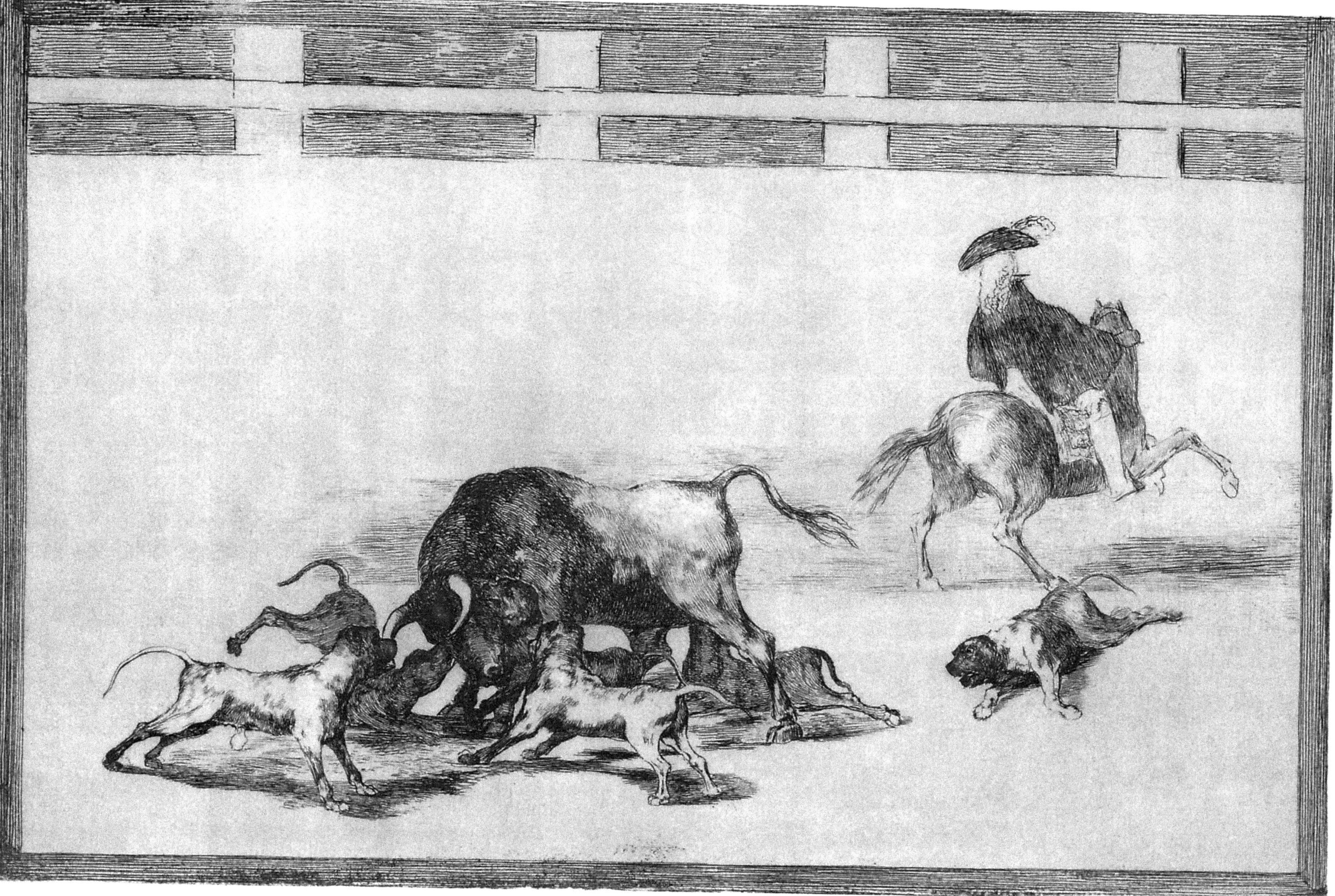

25 ECHAN PERROS AL TORO / *They loose dogs on the bull*

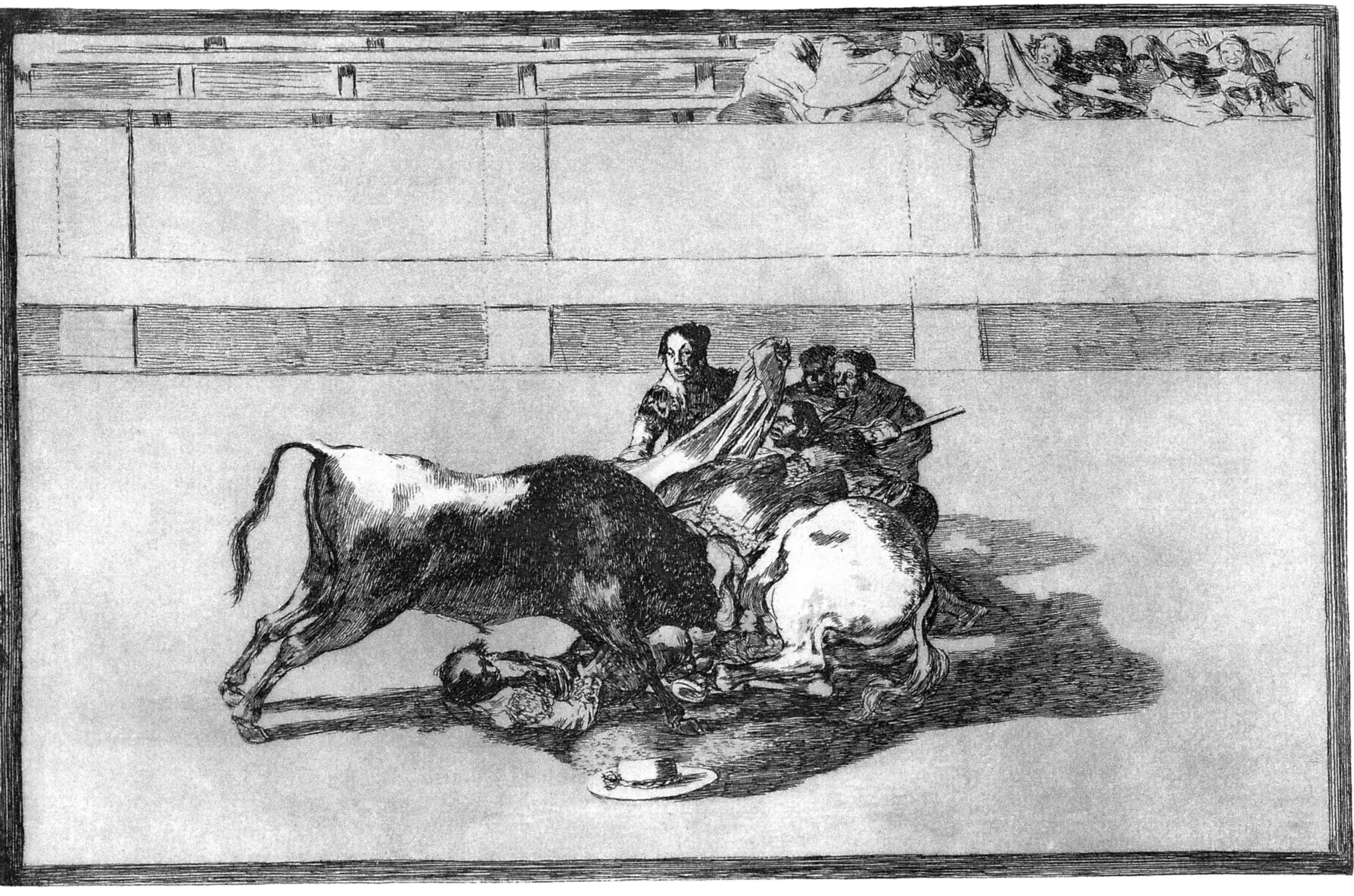

26 Caida de un picador de su caballo debajo del toro / *A picador is unhorsed and falls under the bull*

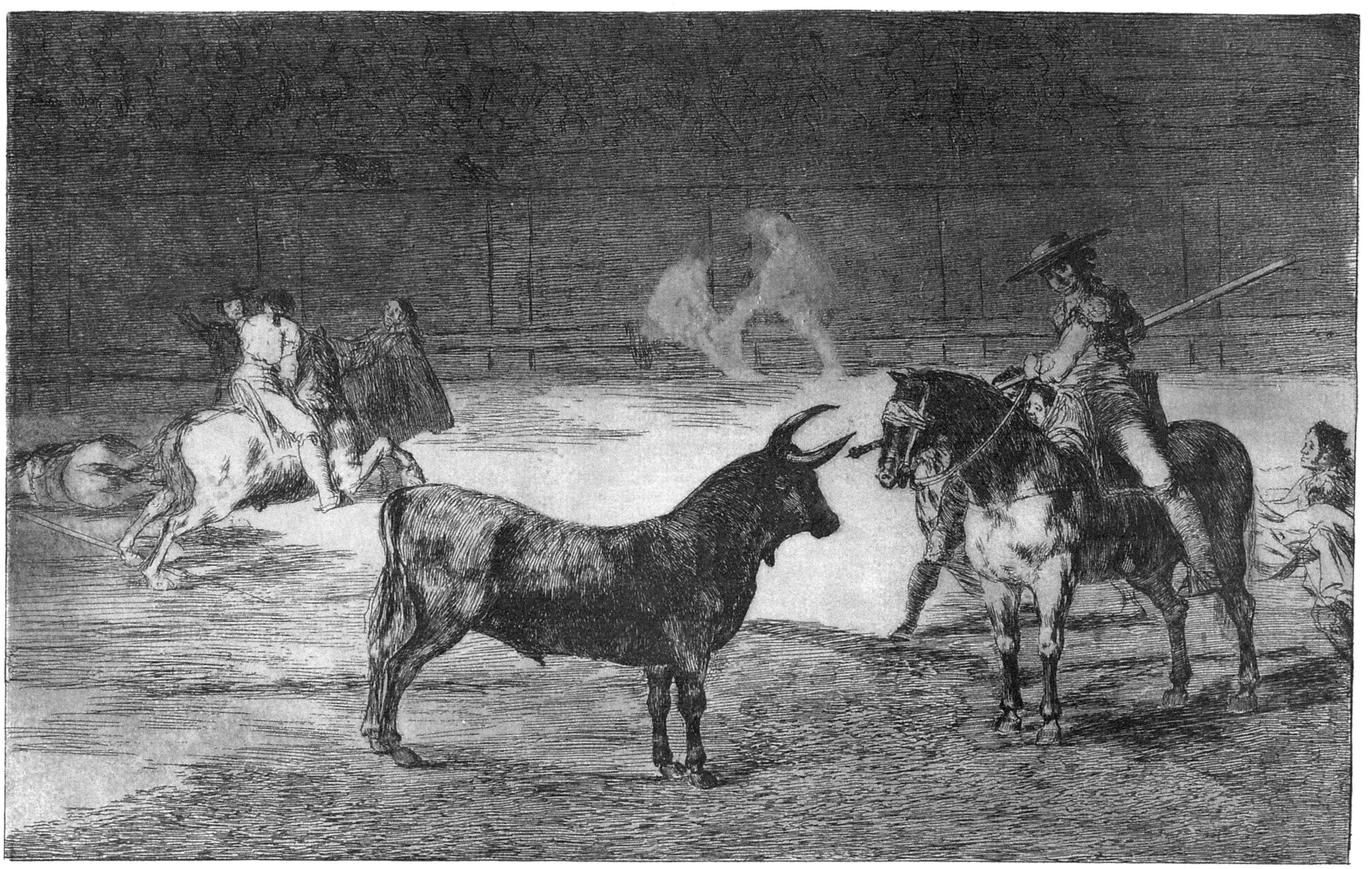

27 El célebre Fernando del Toro, barilarguero, obligando á la fiera con su garrocha / *The celebrated picador, Fernando del Toro, draws the fierce beast on with his pique*

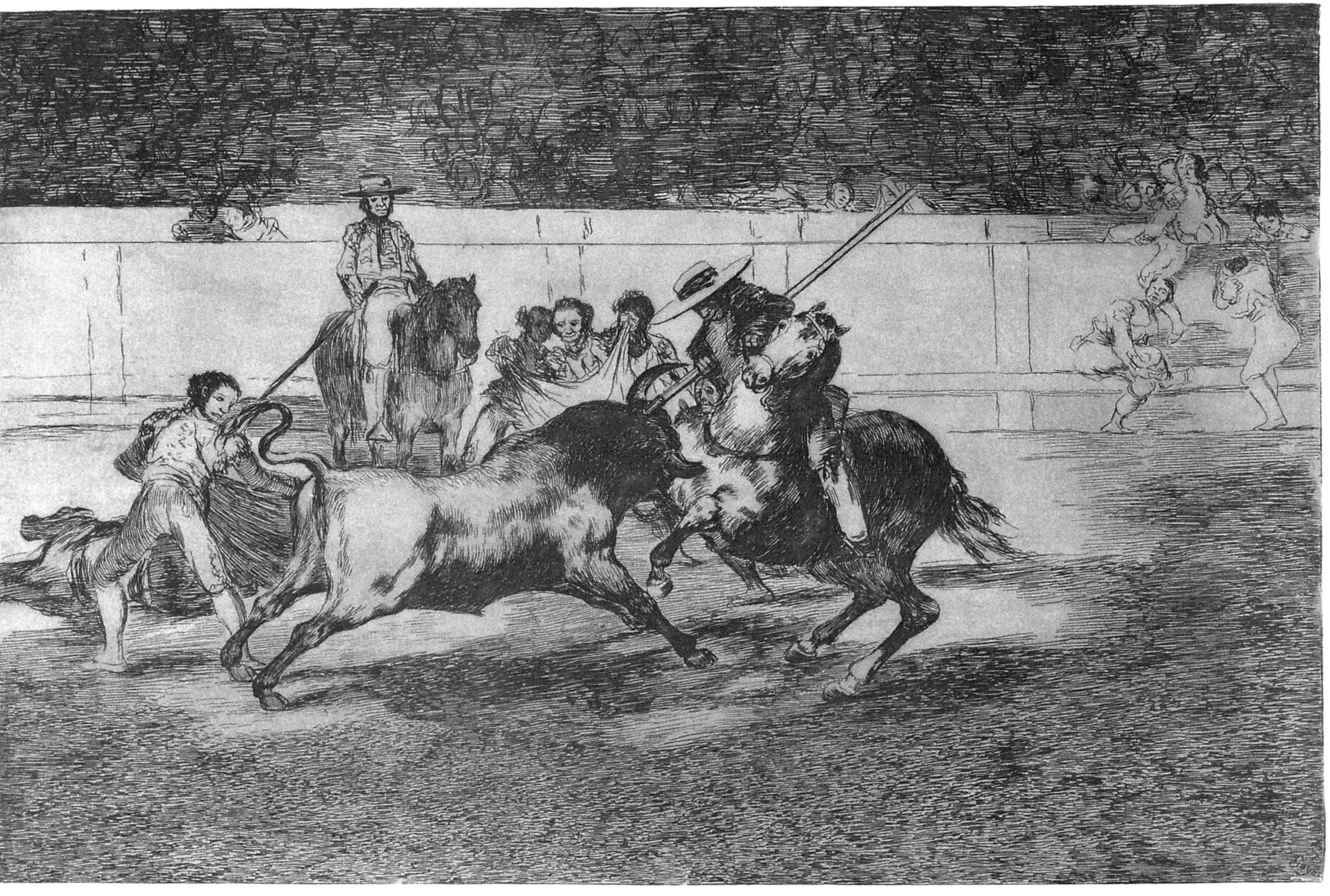

28 El esforzado Rendon picando un toro, de cuya suerte murió en la plaza de Madrid / *The forceful Rendon stabs a bull with the pique, from which pass he died in the ring at Madrid*

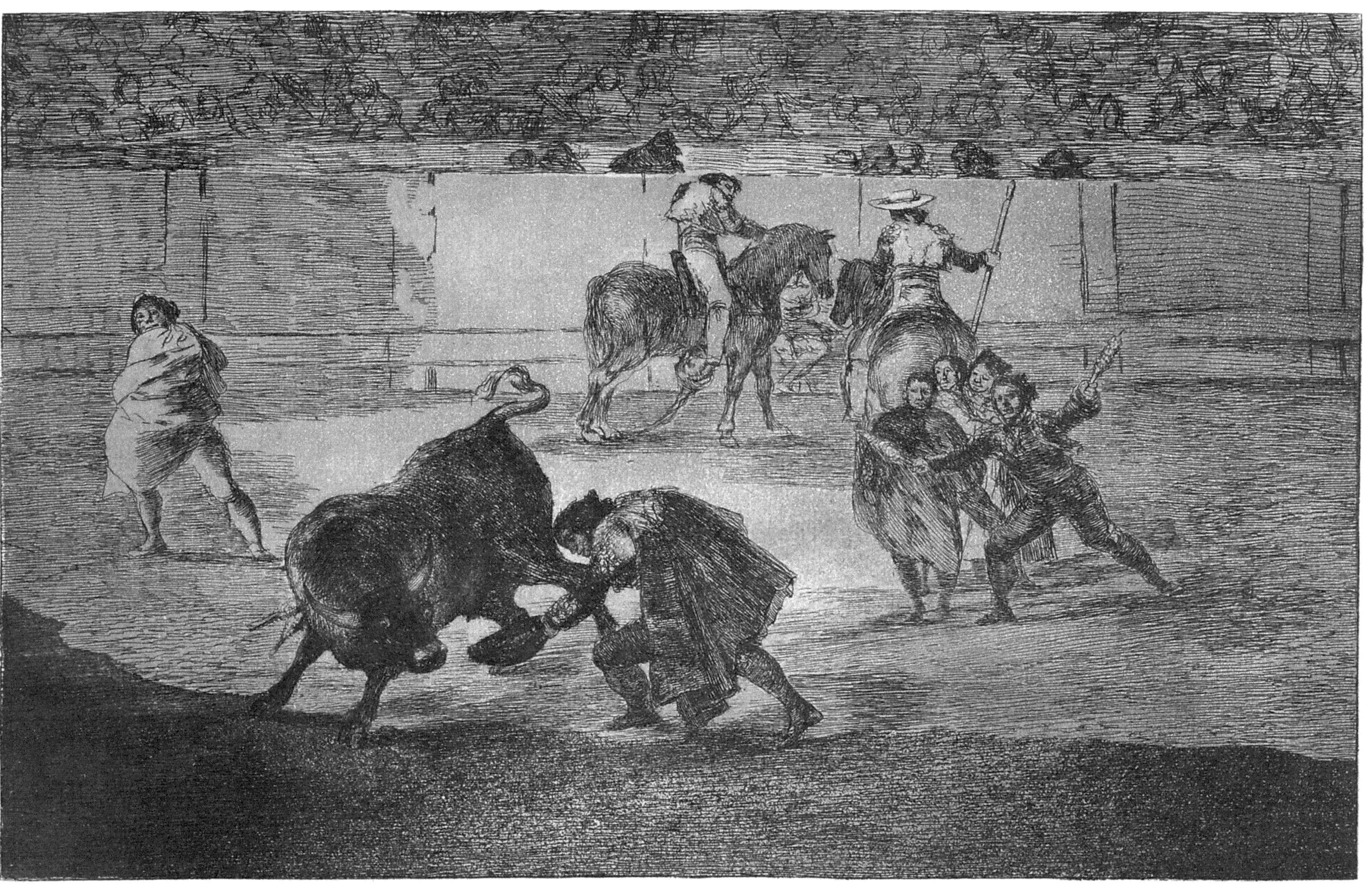

29 Pepe Illo haciendo el recorte al toro / *Pepe Illo making the pass of the "recorte"*

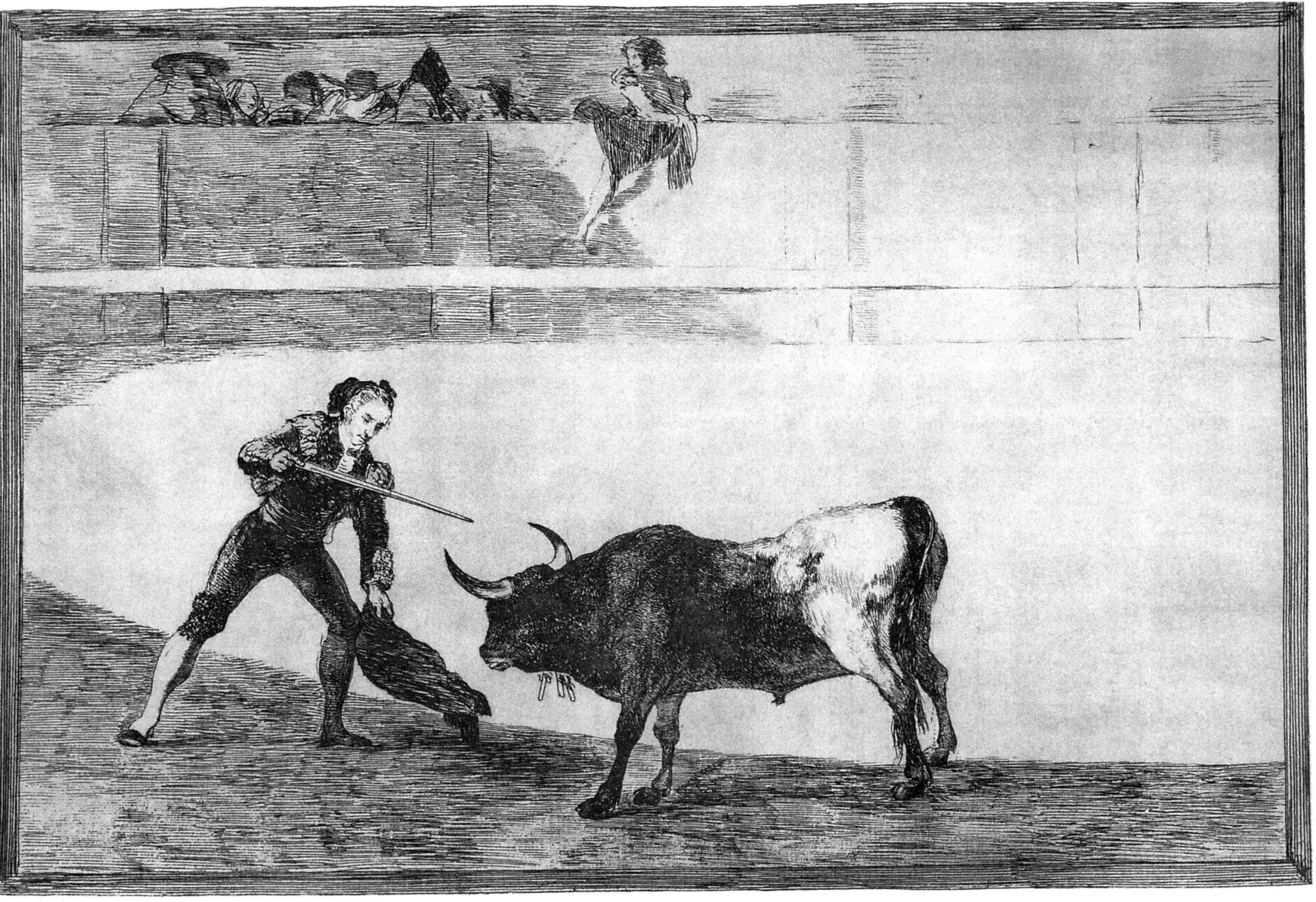

30 Pedro Romero matando á toro parado / *Pedro Romero killing the halted bull*

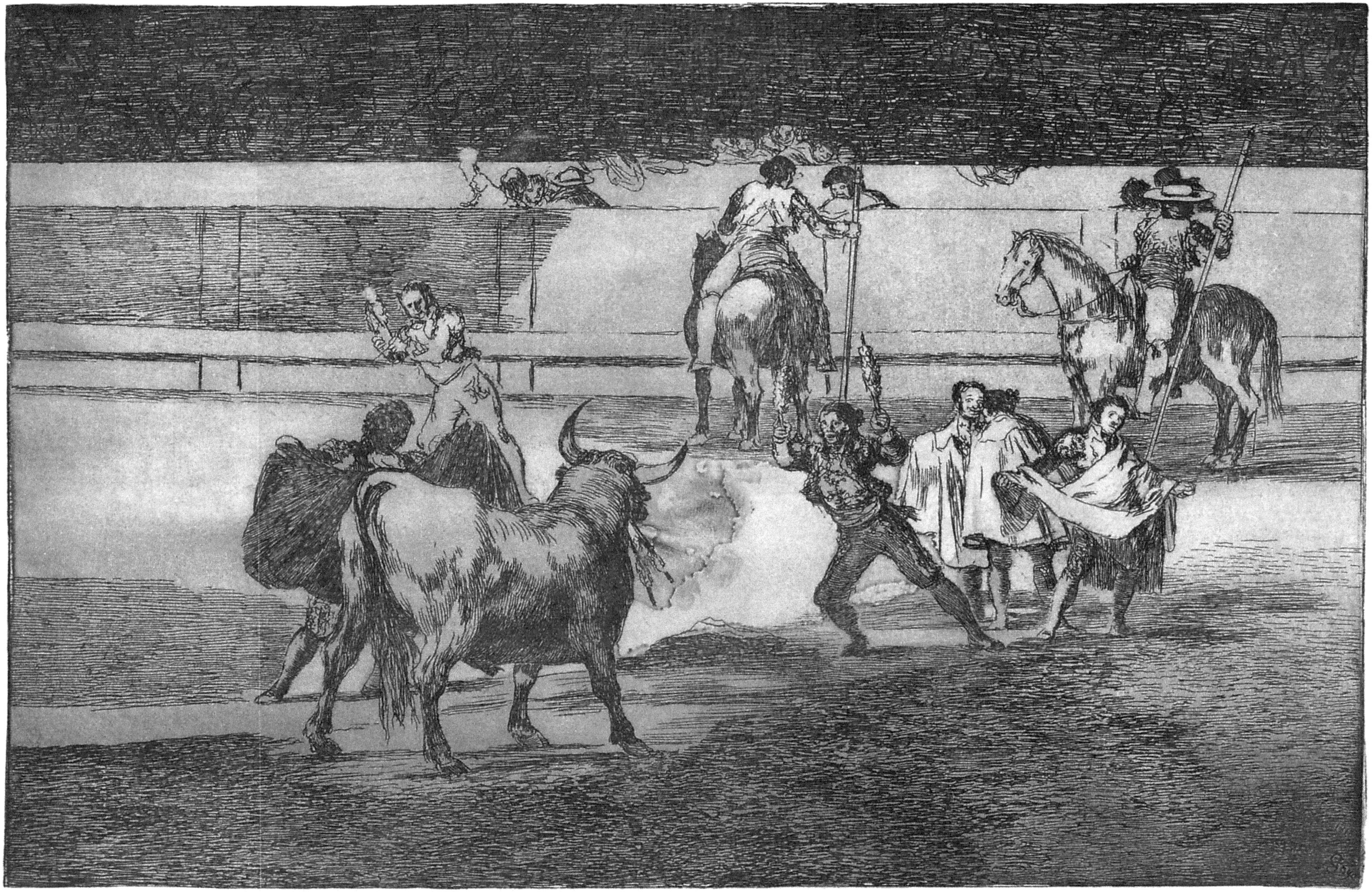

31 BANDERILLAS DE FUEGO / *Banderillas with firecrackers*

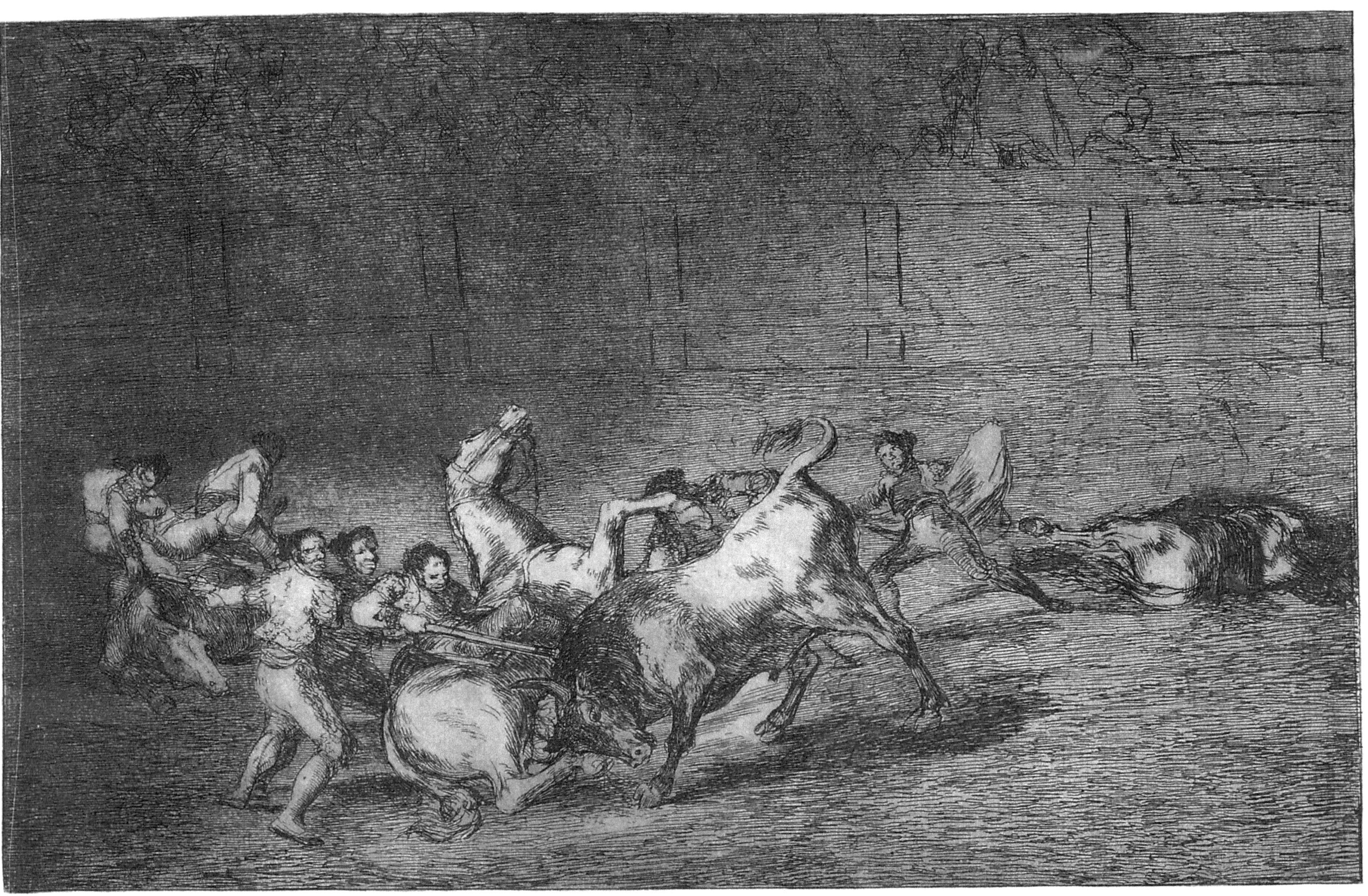

32 Dos grupos de picadores arrollados de seguida por un solo toro / *Two teams of picadors thrown one after the other by a single bull*

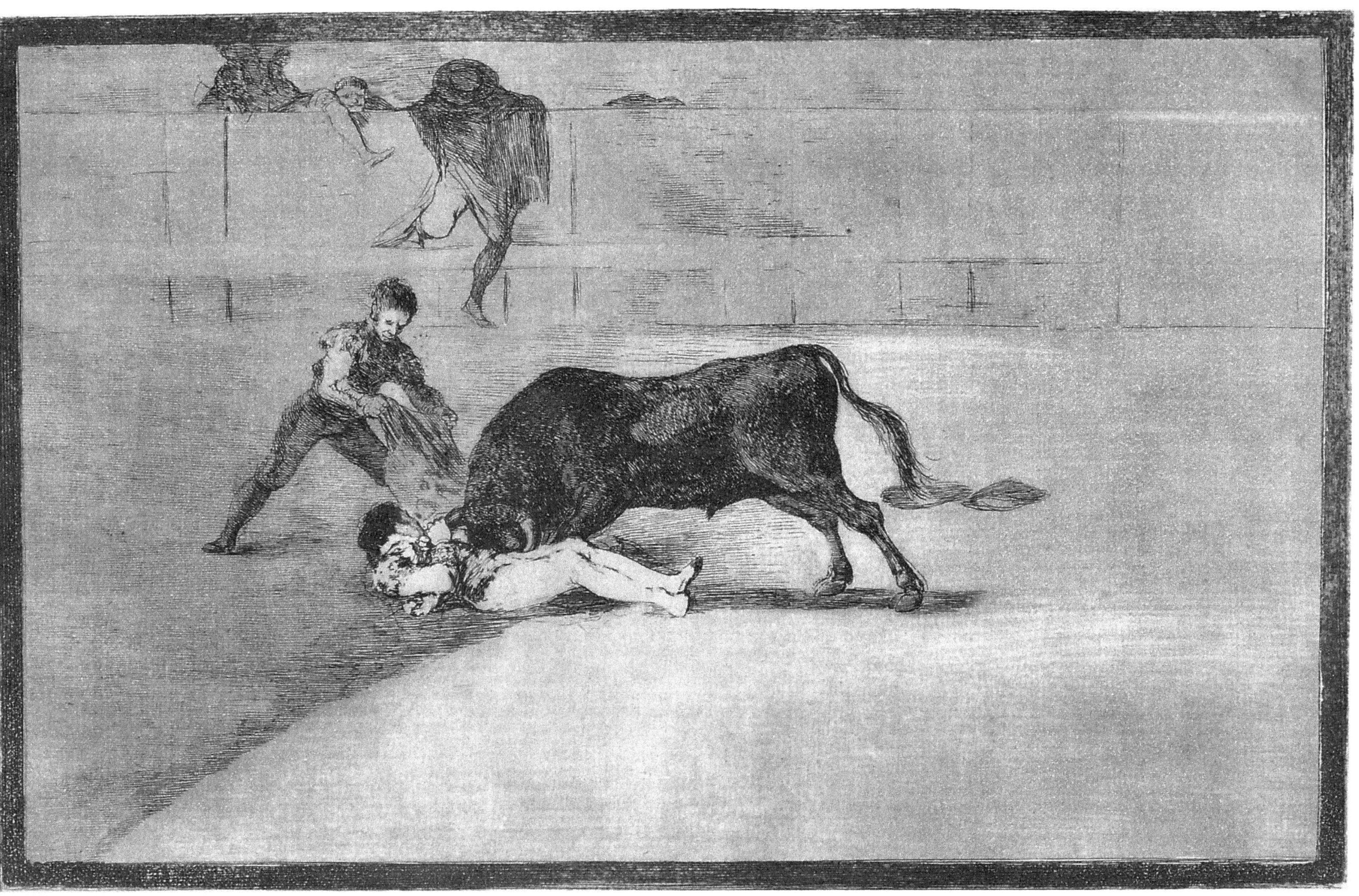

33 La desgraciada muerte de Pepe Illo en la plaza de Madrid / *The unlucky death of Pepe Illo in the ring at Madrid*

LA TAUREAUMACHIE

RECUEIL DE QUARANTE ESTAMPES INVENTÉES ET GRAVÉES A L'EAU-FORTE

PAR DON FRANCISCO GOYA Y LUCIENTES

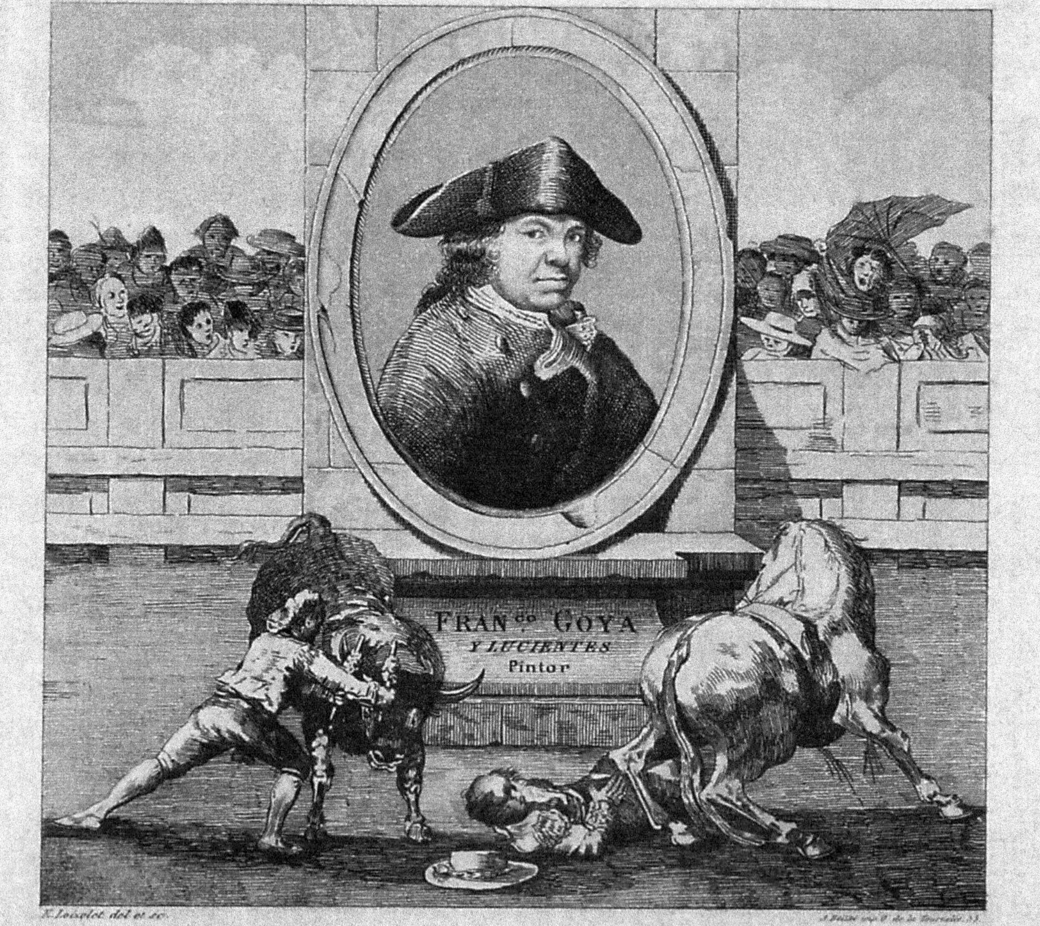

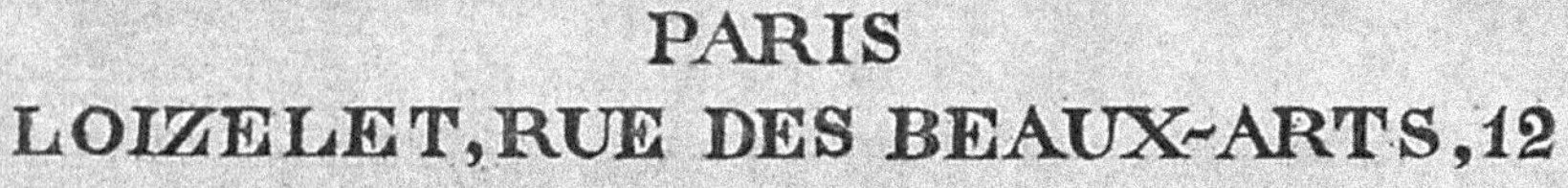

PARIS

LOIZELET, RUE DES BEAUX-ARTS, 12

Title page of first edition (1876) of *Tauromaquia* A–G (etchings by the publisher, Loizelet)

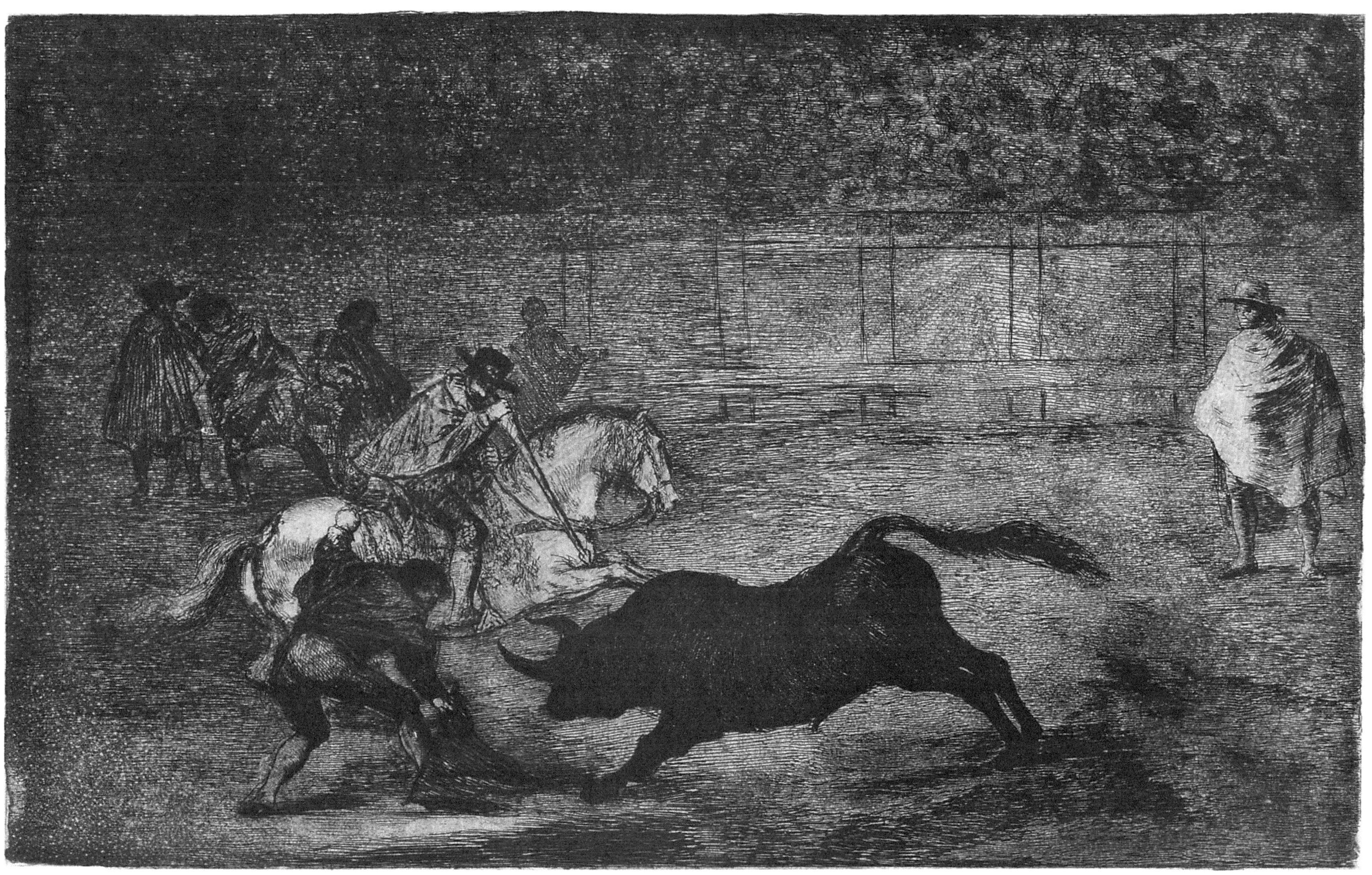

34A Un cavalier espagnol brisant des "rejoncillos" avec l'aide des chulos/*A Spanish mounted knight breaking short spears with the help of assistants*

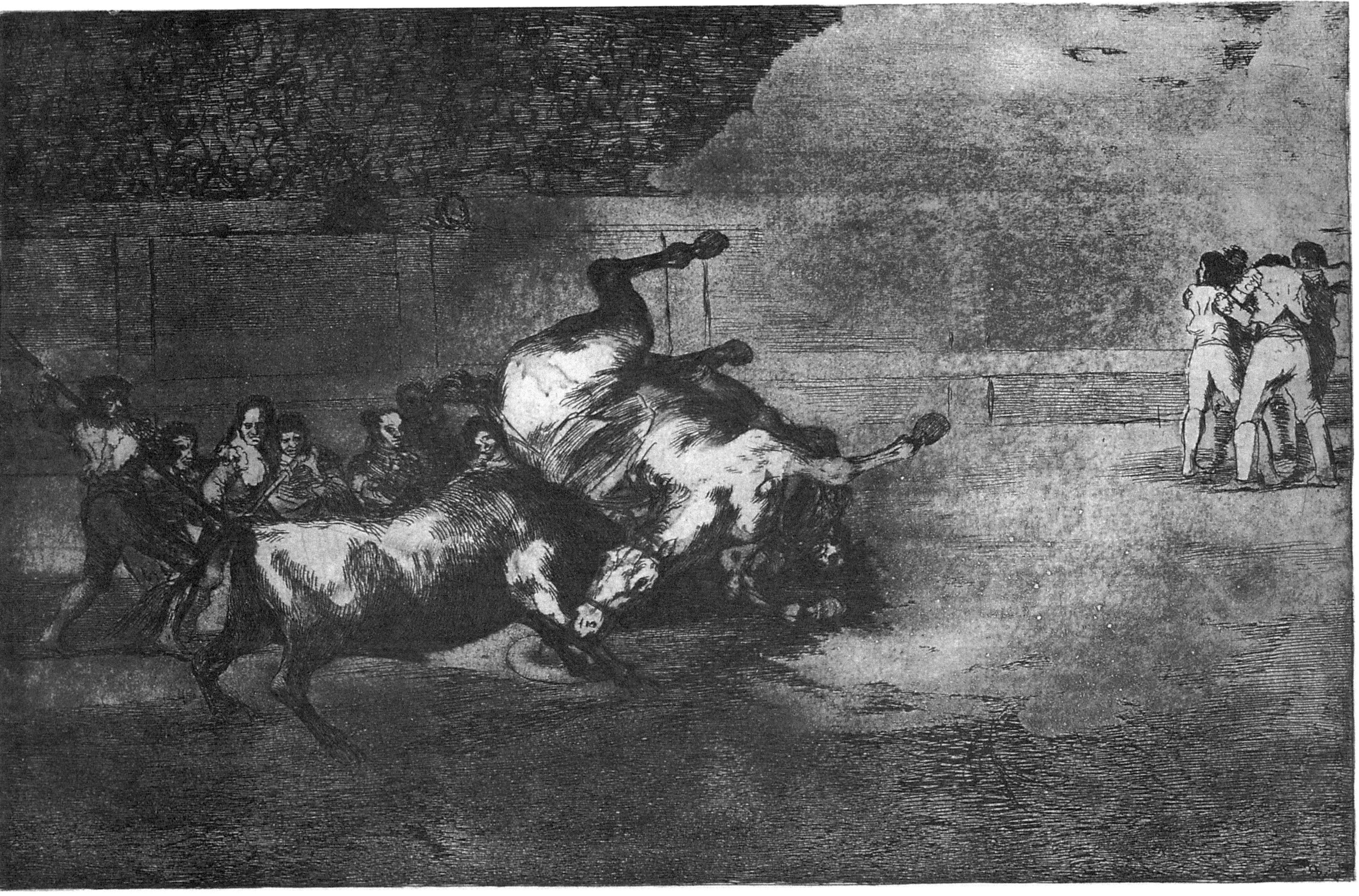

35B CHEVAL RENVERSÉ PAR UN TAUREAU / *Horse thrown by a bull*

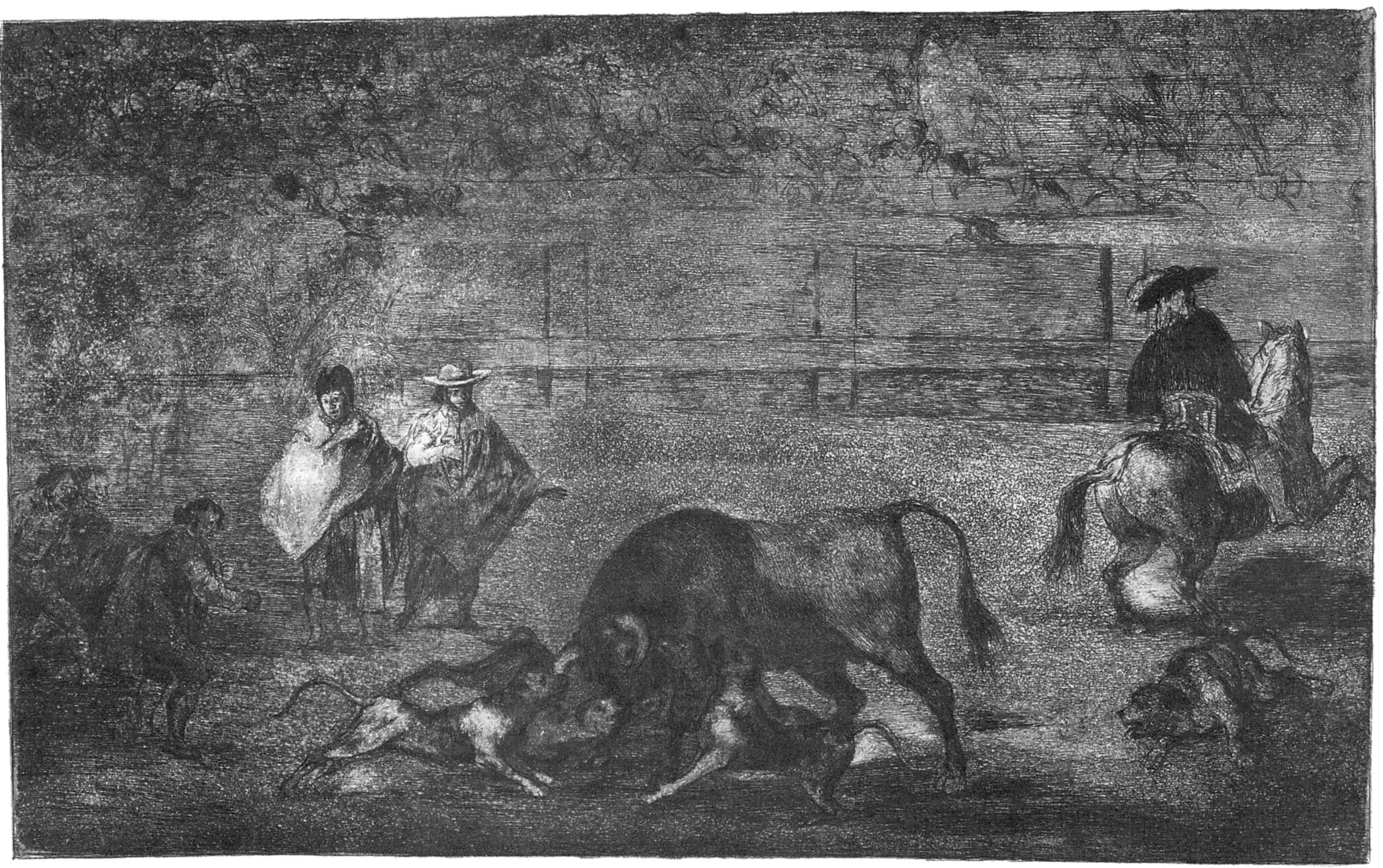

36C LES CHIENS LÂCHÉS SUR LE TAUREAU / *The dogs let loose on the bull*

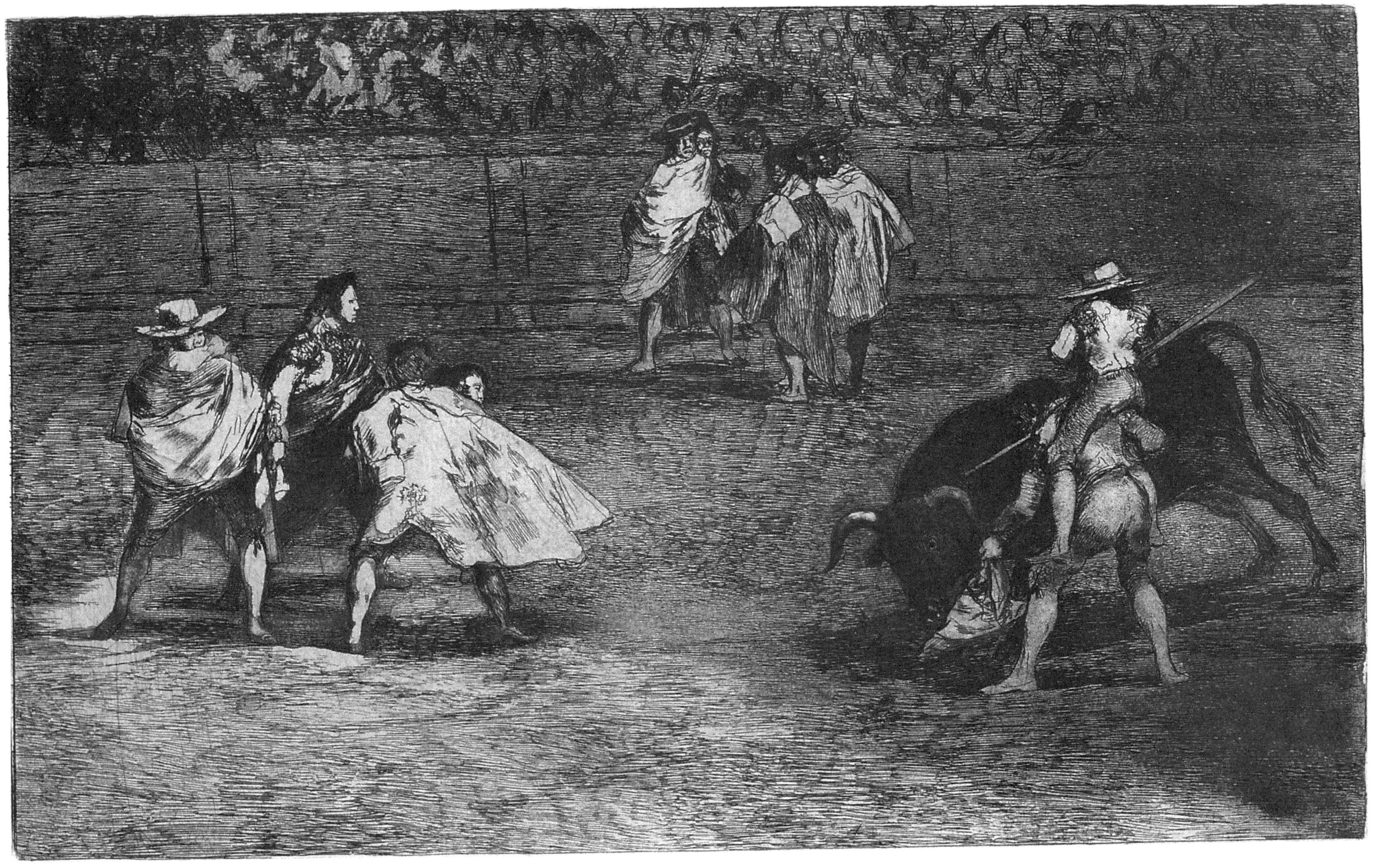

37D Un torero monté sur les épaules d'un chulo "lanceando" un taureau / *A bullfighter, mounted on the shoulders of an assistant, spearing a bull*

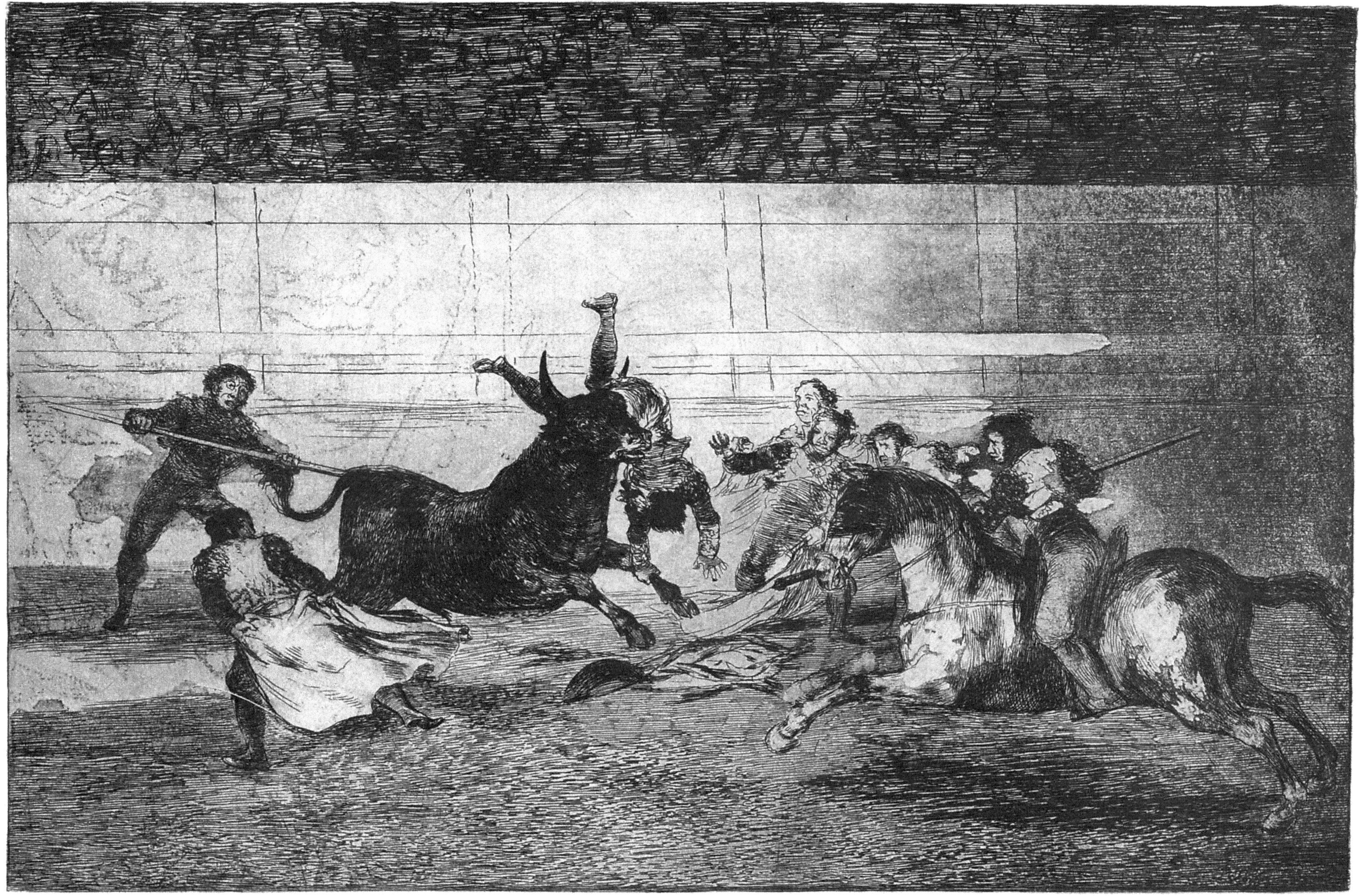

38E Mort de Pepe Illo (2e composition) / *Death of Pepe Illo (2nd composition)*

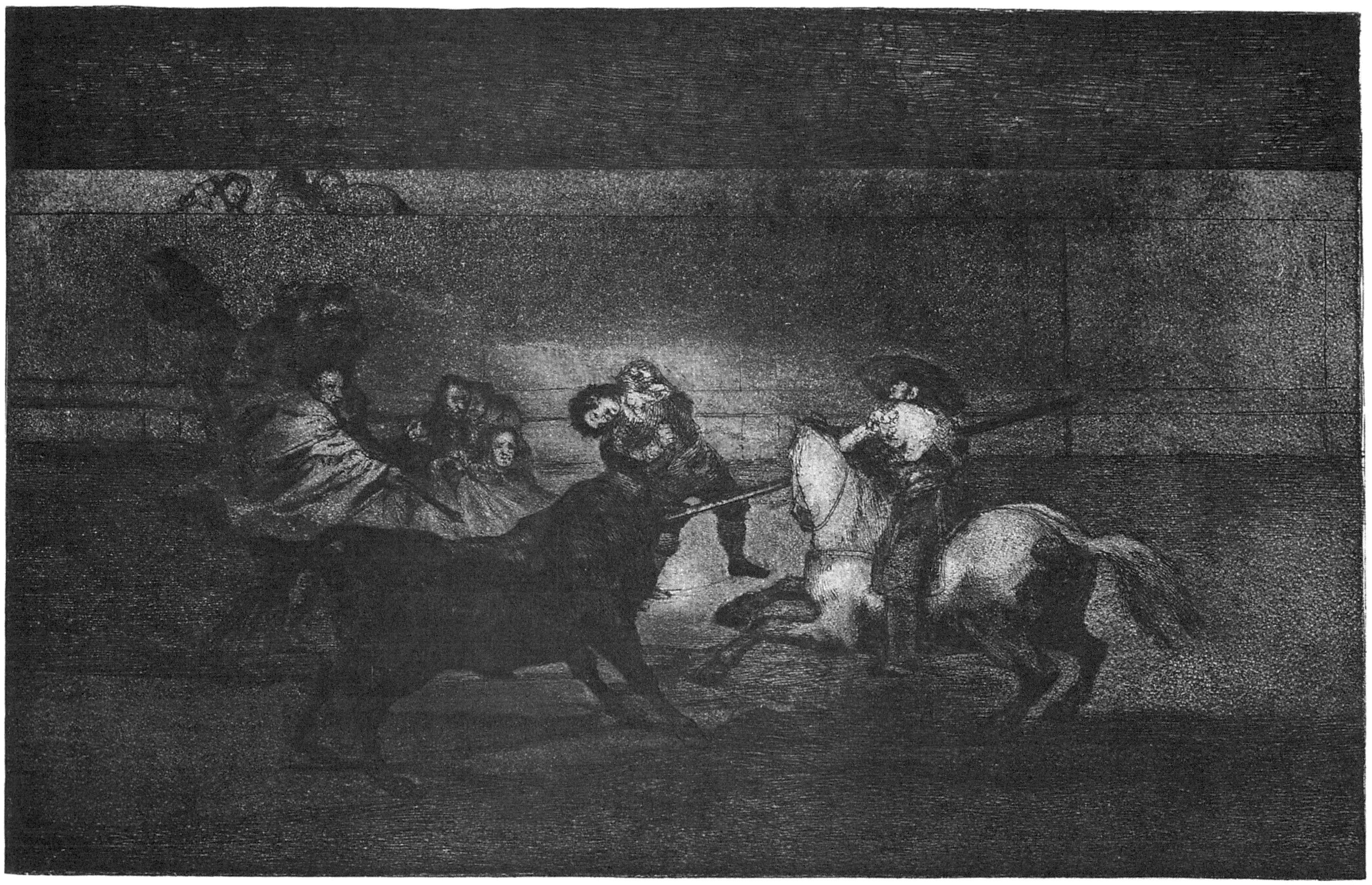

39F Mort de Pepe Illo (3e composition) / *Death of Pepe Illo (3rd composition)*

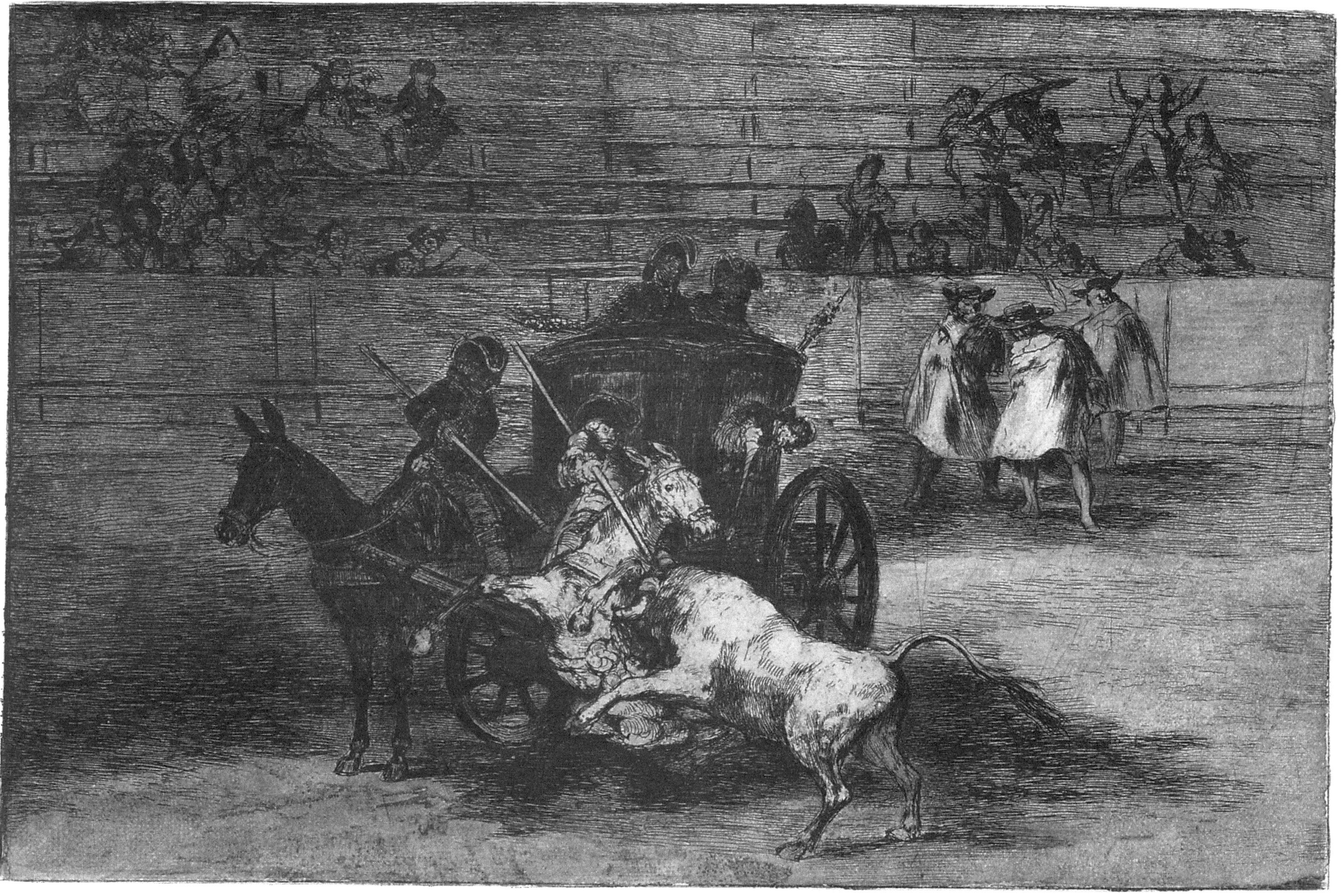

40G Combat dans une voiture attelée de deux mulets / *Fight in a carriage harnessed to two mules*

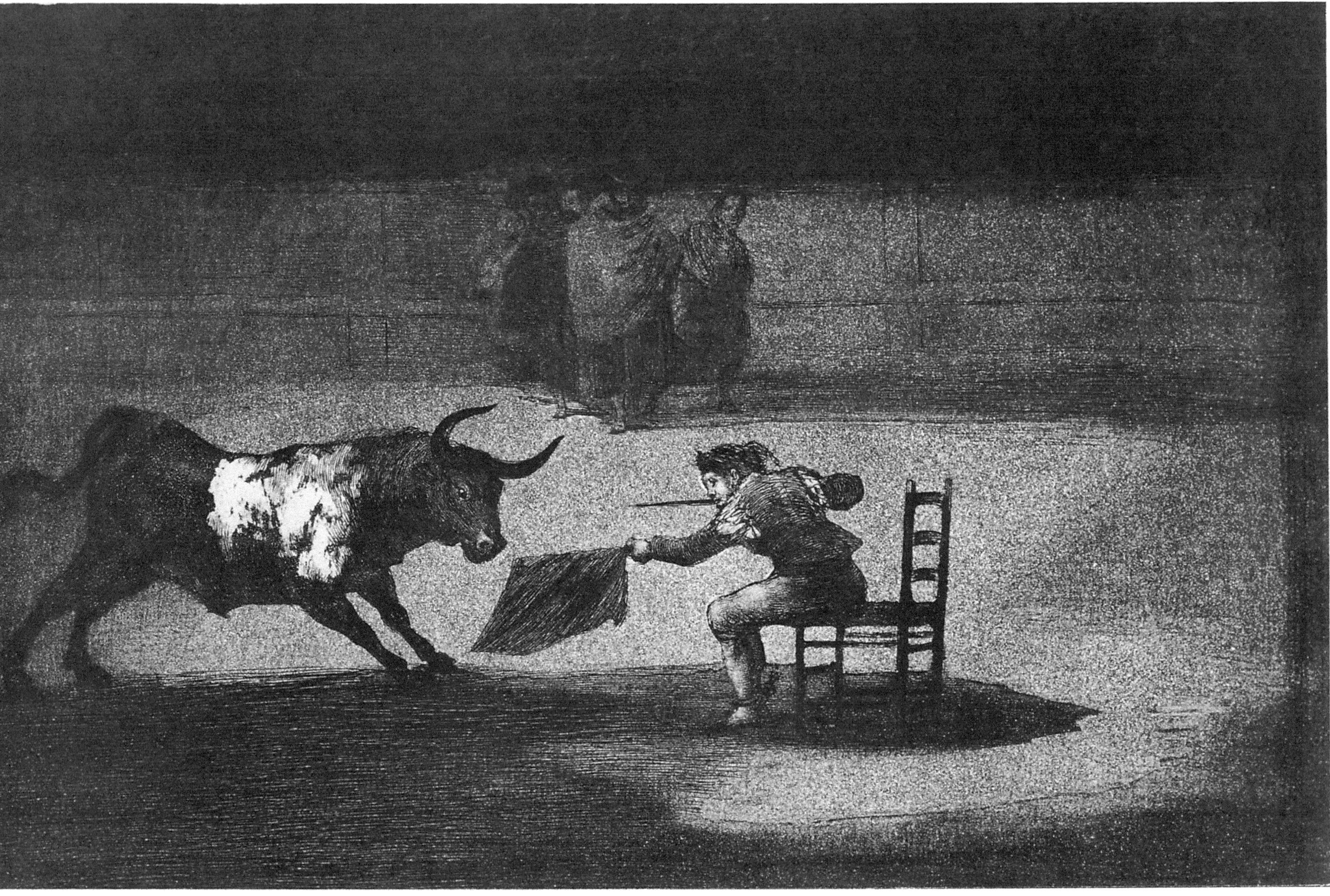

Daring of Martincho in the bullring at Saragossa

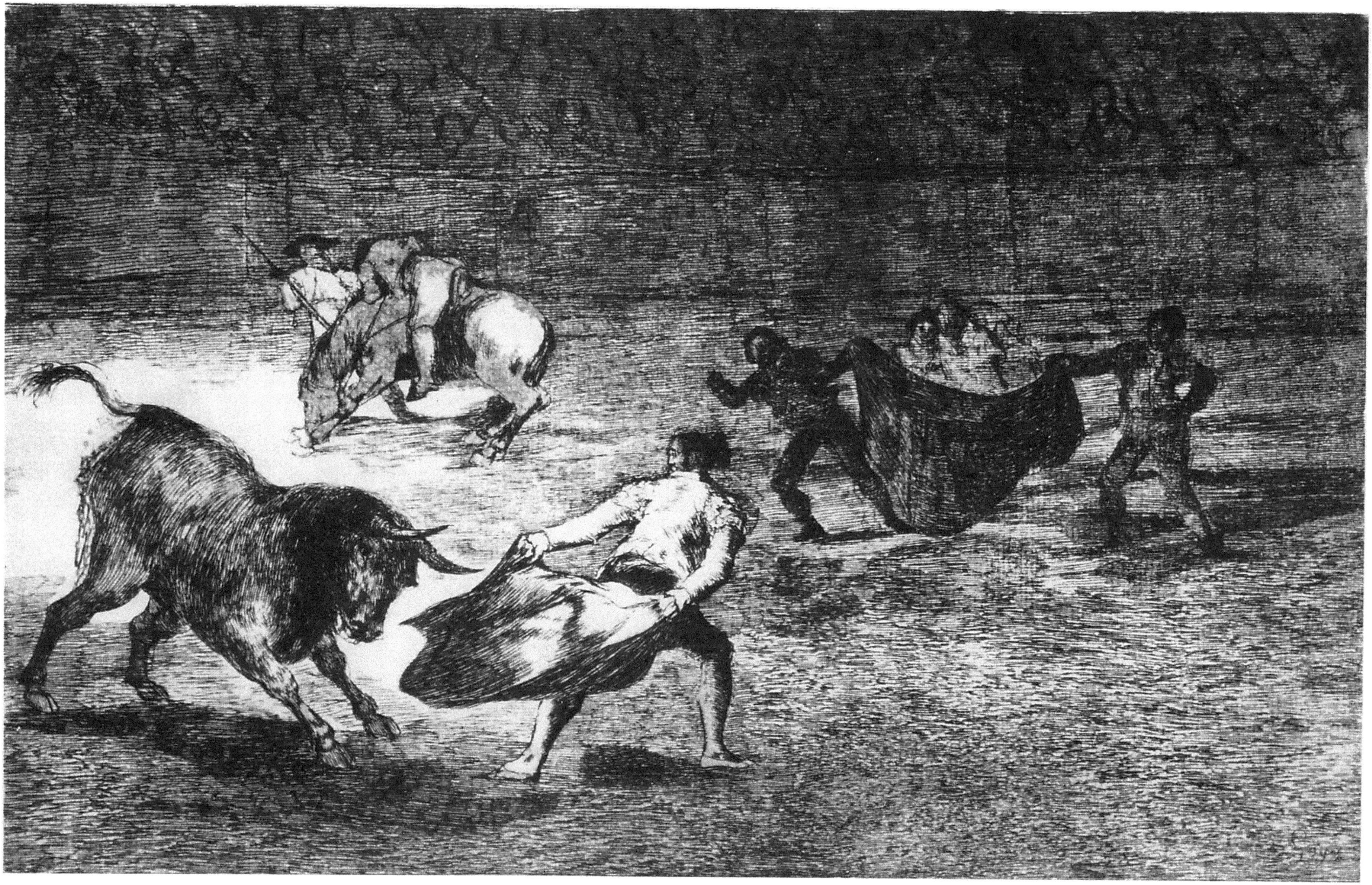

A skillful fighter calling the bull with his back turned

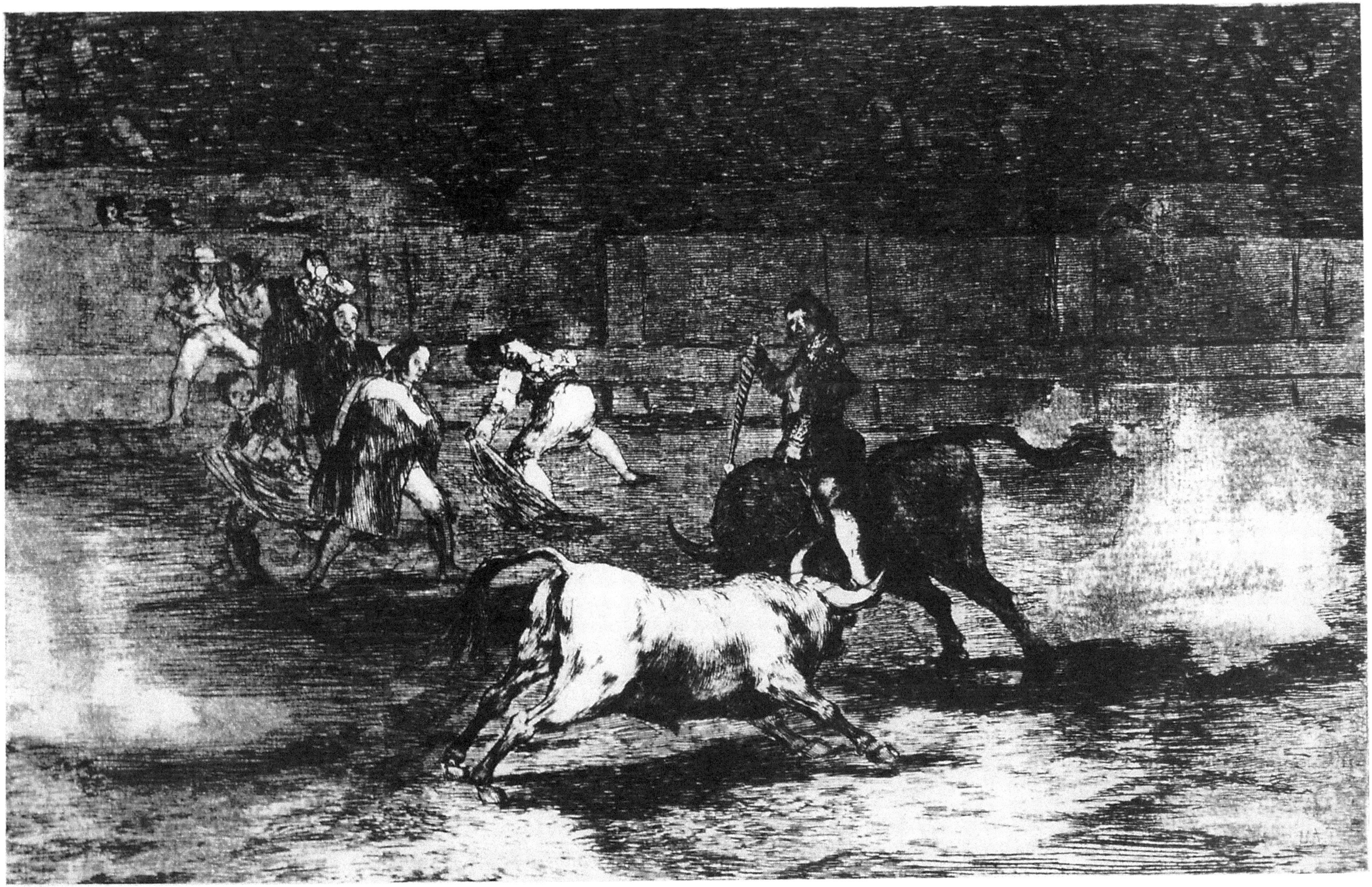

Mariano Ceballos mounted on a bull, breaking spears

The Bulls of Bordeaux

Introduction to The Bulls of Bordeaux

AN AMAZING FACT about Goya in his old age is that his work did not fall off, as so often happens with lesser artists, but even improved. Moreover, he also experimented with a new graphic technique (lithography) from about 1819, when he was already 73 years old, and even invented new subjects and new styles!

Of this last period his most important prints were certainly the four large lithographs, originally measuring 12¼ x 16¼ inches, called popularly *The Bulls of Bordeaux*, because made in that city where Goya had gone in 1824 to join other Spanish liberals in voluntary exile. These four prints (reproduced here from fine early impressions)* were registered at the Dépôt Légal of the Gironde Préfecture in November–December, 1825. All but one exist in two or three states, which proves that Goya was constantly experimenting, never quite satisfied. One hundred impressions are supposed to have been made of each lithograph, but perhaps there were a few more. (A fifth print probably connected with the series is reproduced here from the unique proof in the Musée des Beaux-Arts, Bordeaux.)

"The famous American [meaning Mexican!] Mariano Ceballos" (Delteil, no. 286) and "Spanish entertainment" (Delteil, no. 288) are perhaps the least powerful of this series. But it is hard to differentiate. "Bravo toro" (Delteil, no. 287), and "The divided ring" (Delteil, no. 289) are, by any standards, extraordinary creations. In the first-named there is an astonishing diagonal composition with an intense concentration of emphasis on the bloody scene in the foreground; in "The divided ring" we seem to find for about the first time in Western art the favorite Japanese angle of perspective. But since this print of 1825 antedates any real influence in the West from Japanese prints by nearly half a century, one must admit that perspective is partly due to the nature of the spectators' seats, as well as to Goya's tremendous power of improvisation.

Leandro de Moratín observed in 1825 that Goya was incredibly active for a man in his eightieth year, and "still eager to observe the world about him." It was as if nature, at the end, sought to compensate for his many illnesses and his late development.

Laurent Matheron, Goya's first French biographer, based his 1858 description of Goya's way of making these lithographs on an eyewitness account which rings true. While often quoted, this description can hardly be omitted in any discussion of *The Bulls of Bordeaux* prints. Here is a free English translation: "The artist executed these lithographs on an easel, the stone poised upon it like a canvas. He handled his crayons as if they were brushes, without ever sharpening them, and remained standing throughout—stepping back or coming closer by turns, in order to judge the results. By custom, he covered the whole stone first with a uniform grey crayon tone, and then removed with a scraper the portions he wished to highlight, here a head, or a body, there a horse or a bull. He then returned to the lithographic crayon in order to reënforce the shadows, the muscles, or to outline forms clearly and to give them movement. . . . You might smile if I say that those prints of Goya were really drawn under a magnifying glass. But this is not far from the truth; for his eyesight had begun to fail. . . ."

Could there possibly be a more vivid description of the old artist at work?

Cambridge, Massachusetts
January 1969

PHILIP HOFER

*These are some of the characteristics of the impressions reproduced here: "Mariano Ceballos" has a lithographed caption omitted here for reasons of space; "Bravo toro" does not yet show the reworking in the background over the head of the mounted picador; "The divided ring" is a variant or an undescribed state, the lower margin being unfinished and shelving up noticeably at the right, and with two false lines still protruding from the upper right-hand corner.

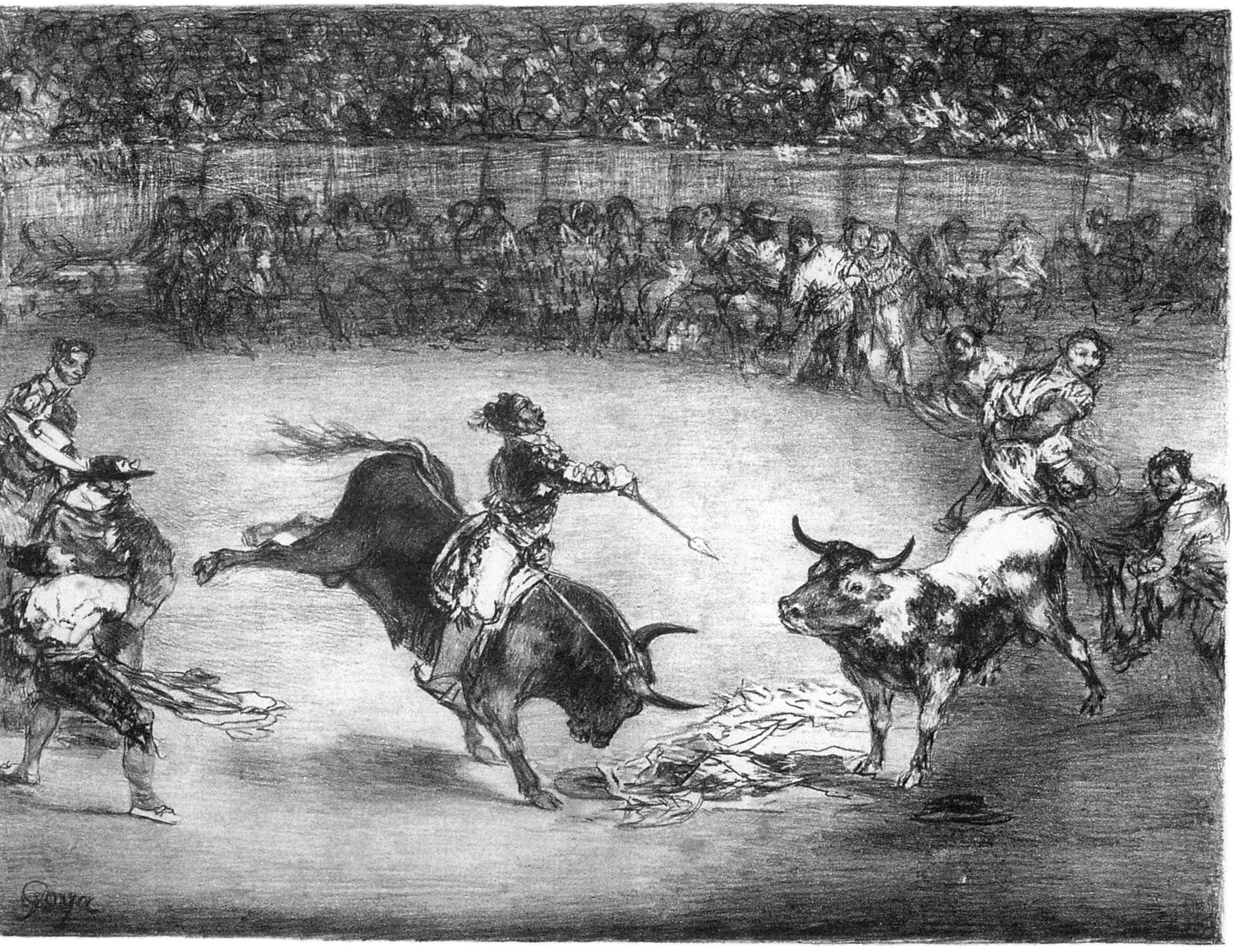

1 El famoso Americano, Mariano Ceballos / *The famous American, Mariano Ceballos*

2 [Bravo toro] / *Picador caught by a bull*

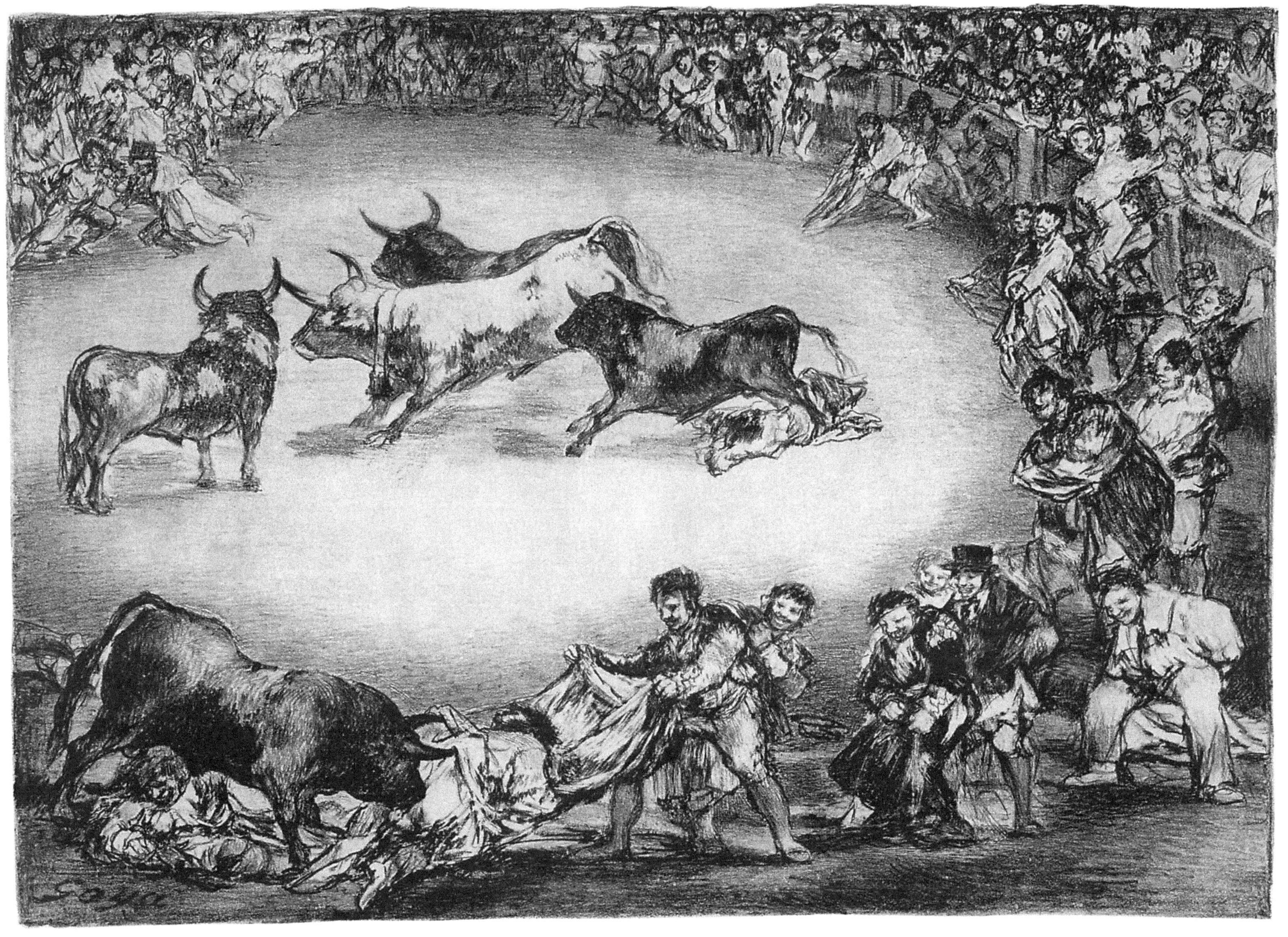

3 DIBERSION DE ESPAÑA / *Spanish entertainment*

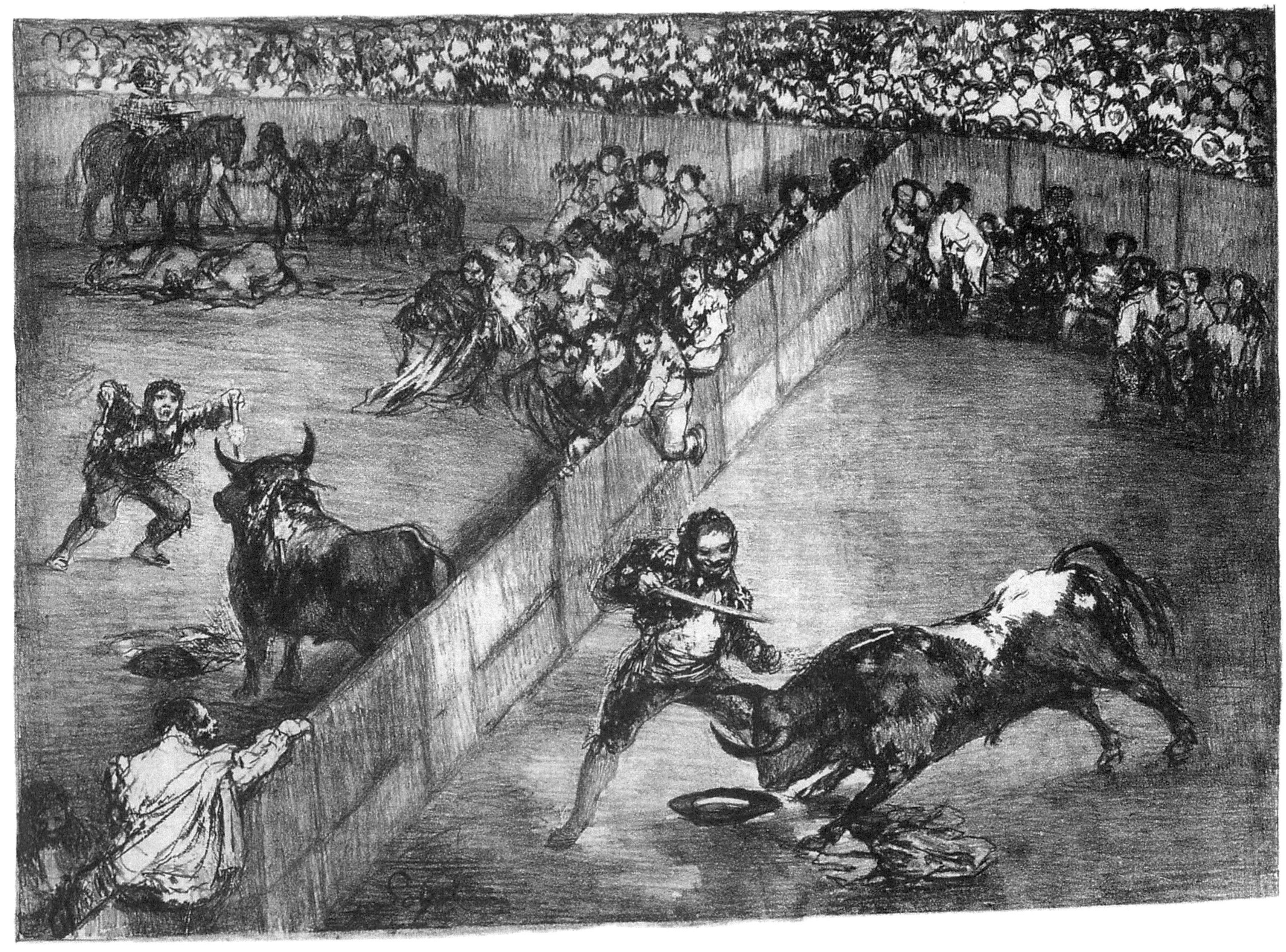

4 *Bullfight in a divided ring*

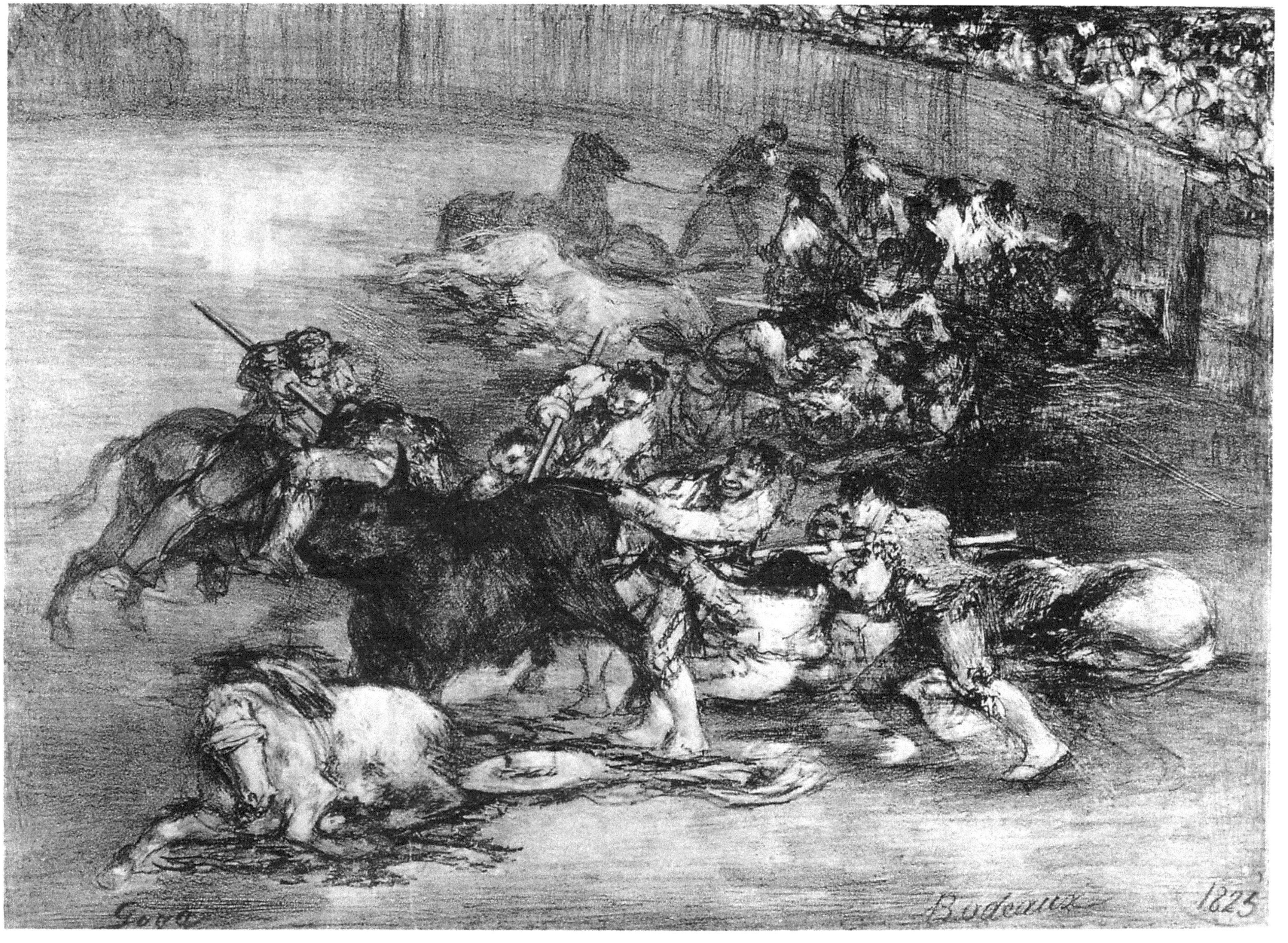

Bullfight